PROBLEM SOLVING

PROBLEM SOLVING

A HANDBOOK FOR TEACHERS

Second Edition

Stephen Krulik

Jesse A. Rudnick

Temple University

Allyn and Bacon, Inc.

Boston, London, Sydney, Toronto

Library of Congress Cataloging-in-Publication Data

Krulik, Stephen.
  Problem solving.

  Bibliography: p.
  1. Problem solving.   I. Rudnick, Jesse A.   II. Title.
[QA63.K78 1987]   153.4'3   86-17463
ISBN 0-205-10289-1

Printed in the United States of America

10 9 8 7 6 5 4 3 2 1   91 90 89 88 87 86

Contents

Contents

Preface

During the past decade, problem solving has become a major focus of the mathematics curriculum. In this era of technology, it is more important than ever for our students to learn how to approach a problem situation.

This book is designed to help you—whether you are a novice or an experienced classroom teacher—to teach *problem solving*. Ever since mathematics has been considered a school subject, the teaching of problem solving has been an enigma to mathematics teachers at all levels, whose efforts to teach students to become better problem solvers seem to have had little effect.

A major portion of the book is devoted to activities and carefully discussed non-routine problems that your students will find interesting as they gain valuable experience in problem solving. The activities and problems have been gleaned from a variety of sources and have been classroom-tested at many levels by practicing teachers. We believe that this is the first time such an expansive set of problems has appeared in a single resource.

Problem solving is now considered to be a basic skill of school mathematics. However, we suggest that it is more than a single skill; rather, it is a group of several discrete skills. Thus in the chapter on pedagogy the subskills of problem solving are enumerated and then integrated into a teachable process. The chapter is highlighted by a flowchart that guides students through this vital process. Although there are many publications that deal with the problem-solving process, we believe that this is the first one that focuses on these subskills.

We are confident that this book will prove to be a valuable asset in your efforts to teach problem solving.

S.K. and J.R.

CHAPTER ONE

An Introduction to Problem Solving

WHAT IS A PROBLEM?

A major difficulty in discussing problem solving seems to be a lack of any clear-cut agreement as to what constitutes a "problem." A problem is a situation, quantitative or otherwise, that confronts an individual or group of individuals, that requires resolution, and for which the individual sees no apparent or obvious means or path to obtaining the solution.

The key to this definition is the phrase "no apparent or obvious . . . path." As children pursue their mathematical training, what were problems at an early age become exercises and are eventually reduced to mere questions. We distinguish between these three commonly used terms as follows:

(a) question: a situation that can be resolved by mere recall.
(b) exercise: a situation that involves drill and practice to reinforce a previously learned skill or algorithm.
(c) problem: a situation that requires thought and a synthesis of previously learned knowledge to resolve.

In addition, a problem must be perceived as such by a student, regardless of the reason, in order to be considered a problem by him or her. Thus a problem must satisfy the following three criteria, illustrated in Figure 1-1.

1. *Acceptance:* The individual accepts the problem. There is a personal involvement which may be due to any of a variety of reasons, including internal motivation, external motivation (peer, parent, and/or teacher pressure), or simply the desire to experience the enjoyment of solving a problem.
2. *Blockage:* The individual's initial attempts at solution are fruitless. His or her habitual responses and patterns of attack do not work.
3. *Exploration:* The personal involvement identified in (1) forces the individual to explore new methods of attack.

Acceptance   Blockage   Exploration

Figure 1-1

3

The existence of a problem implies that the individual is confronted by something he or she does not recognize, and to which he or she cannot merely apply a model. A problem will no longer be considered a problem once it can easily be solved by algorithms that have been previously learned.

A word about textbook problems: While most mathematics textbooks contain sections labeled "verbal problems," not all are really problems. In many cases, a model solution has already been presented in class by the teacher. The student merely applies this model to the series of similar "problems" in order to solve them. Essentially the student is learning an algorithm—a technique that applies to a single class of "problems" and that guarantees success if mechanical errors are avoided. Few of these so-called problems require higher-order thought by the students. Yet the first time a student sees these "verbal problems," they could be problems to him or her, if presented in a non-algorithmic fashion. Students want to solve them because the work has been assigned by the teacher, or because they need to obtain a good grade in the course. And students may experience blockage and frustration.

We consider these "verbal problems" to be "exercises," or "routine problems." This is not to say that we advocate removing them from the curriculum. They do serve a purpose, and for this purpose they should be retained. They provide exposure to problem situations, practice in the use of the algorithm, and drill in the associated mathematical processes. However, a teacher should not think that students who have been solving these exercises through use of a carefully developed model or algorithm have been exposed to problem solving.

WHAT IS PROBLEM SOLVING?

Problem solving is a process. It is the means by which an individual uses previously acquired knowledge, skills, and understanding to satisfy the demands of an unfamiliar situation. The student must synthesize what he or she has learned, and apply it to the new and different situation.

Some educators assume that expertise in problem solving develops incidentally as one solves many problems. While this may be true in part, we feel that problem-solving skills should be considered as a distinct body of knowledge, and should be taught as such.

The knowledge of mathematics can be divided into several parts, two of which are (1) information and facts and (2) the ability to use information and facts. This ability to use information and facts is an essential part of the problem-solving process. In effect, problem solving requires analysis and synthesis. To succeed in problem solving is to learn how to learn.

WHY TEACH PROBLEM SOLVING?

In dealing with the issue of why we should teach problem solving, we must first consider the larger question: Why teach mathematics? The majority of students will rarely use pure higher mathematics in their everyday lives, but they will be required to solve quantitative problems that they meet in their social and working day. In almost every instance these quantitative situations will appear as problems. Rarely if ever are people confronted by situations that can be handled readily by the use of an algorithm. For most people, mathematics *is* problem solving!

In spite of the obvious relationship between mathematics of the classroom and the quantitative situations in life, we know that children of all ages see little connection between what happens in school and what happens in real life. An emphasis on problem solving in the classroom can lessen the gap between the real world and the classroom world and thus set a positive mood in the classroom.

In many mathematics classes, students do not see any connections among the various ideas taught during the semester's course of study. Most regard each topic as a separate entity. Problems show the interconnections among mathematical ideas. They are never solved in a vacuum, but are related in some way to something seen before, to something learned earlier. Thus good problems can be used to review past mathematical ideas, as well as to sow seeds for ideas to be presented at a future time.

Problem solving is more exciting, more challenging, and more interesting to children than barren exercises. If we examine student performance in the classroom, we recognize the obvious fact that success leads to persistence and continuation of a task; failure leads to avoidance. It is this continuance that we constantly strive for in mathematics. The greater the involvement, the better the end product. Thus a carefully selected sequence of problem-solving activities that yield success will stimulate students, leading them to a more positive attitude toward mathematics in general, and problem solving in particular.

Finally, problem solving permits students to learn and to practice heuristic thinking. A careful selection of problems is a major vehicle by which we provide a "sharpening" of problem-solving skills and strategies so necessary in real life.

WHEN DO WE TEACH PROBLEM SOLVING?

Since the process of problem solving is a teachable skill, when do we teach it? What does it replace? Where does it fit into the day-to-day schedule?

Experiences in problem solving are always at hand. All other activities are subservient. Thus the teaching of problem solving should occur in virtually every class period. Discussion of problems, proposed solutions, methods of attacking problems, etc., should be considered at all times. Think how poorly students would perform in other skill areas, such as fractions, if they were taught these skills in one or two weeks of concentrated work and then the skills were never used.

Naturally there will be times when studies of algorithmic skills and drill and practice sessions will be called for. These times will permit the delay necessary for the incubation period required by many problems, which need time to "set." By allowing time between problem-solving sessions, you permit students to become familiar with the problem-solving process slowly, and over a longer period of time.

The number of problems discussed in any one class session must, of necessity, be small. This is a natural outgrowth of the process of problem solving. The goals are a study of the problem-solving process and growth in using this process, rather than merely "covering material."

WHAT MAKES A GOOD PROBLEM SOLVER?

Although we cannot easily determine what it is that makes some students good problem solvers, there are certain common characteristics exhibited by good problem solvers. For one thing, a good problem solver has a *desire* to solve problems. Problems interest him or her; they offer a challenge. Much like climbers of Mt. Everest, problem solvers like to solve problems because they exist.

Problem solvers are extremely *perseverant* when solving problems. They are not easily discouraged when incorrect, or when a particular approach leads to a dead end. They go back and try new approaches again and again. They refuse to quit!

If one method of attacking a problem fails to yield a satisfactory solution, successful problem solvers try another. A variety of methods of attack are usually at their disposal. They will often try the opposite of what they have been doing in the hope that new information will occur to them. They will ask themselves many "What if . . ." questions, changing the problem as they proceed.

Good problem solvers show an ability to skip some of the steps in the solution process. They make connections quickly, notice irrelevant detail, and often require only a few examples in order to generalize. They often show a marked lack of concern about neatness while developing their solution process.

Above all, good problem solvers are not afraid to guess! They will make "educated guesses" at solutions, and then attempt to verify these guesses. They will gradually refine their guesses on the basis of what previous guesses show them, until they find a satisfactory solution. They rarely guess wildly, but use their own intuition to make carefully thought through guesses.

We would suggest that good problem solvers are students who hold conversations with themselves. They know what questions to ask themselves, and what to do with the answers they receive as they think through the problem.

WHAT MAKES A GOOD PROBLEM?

It should be apparent to the reader that we consider problems to be the basic medium of problem solving. Furthermore, problem solving is the basic skill of mathematics education. It follows, then, that without "good" problems we could not have creative mathematics.

What constitutes a good problem? First of all, teachers should be aware that good problems can be found in every branch of mathematics. Problems need not be word problems in order to be good problems, and good problems can be found in virtually every aspect of daily living. What follows in this section are some characteristics of good mathematics problems, together with examples which illustrate these characteristics. Keep in mind that not every good problem need have all of these characteristics. Neither is it always possible to clearly identify which characteristics make a problem good for problem solving—in many cases the characteristics will overlap. However, a good problem will always have some of these attributes.

1. The solution to the problem involves the understanding of a distinct mathematical concept or the use of a mathematical skill.

Many problems appear to be non-mathematical in context, yet the solution to the problems involves basic mathematical principles. Perhaps a pattern can be found that the students recognize. Or some application of a skill may quickly resolve the problem. In any case, there should be some basic mathematical skill and/or concept imbedded in the problem and its solution.

PROBLEM   The new school has exactly 1,000 lockers and exactly 1,000 students. On the first day of school, the students meet outside the building and agree on the following plan: The first student will enter the school and open all of the lockers. The second student will then enter the school and close every locker with an even number (2, 4, 6, 8, . . .). The third student will then "reverse" every third locker. That is, if the locker is closed, he will open it; if the locker is open, he will close it. The fourth student will reverse every fourth locker, and so on until all 1,000 students in turn have entered the building and reversed the proper lockers. Which lockers will finally remain open?

Discussion   It seems rather futile to attempt this experiment with 1,000 lockers, so let's take a look at 20 lockers and 20 students and try to find a pattern.

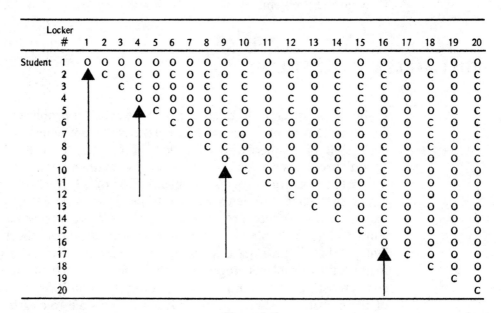

Figure 1-2

In our smaller illustration in Figure 1-2, the lockers with numbers 1, 4, 9, and 16 remain open, while all others are closed. Thus we conclude that those lockers with numbers that are perfect squares will remain open when the process has been completed by all 1,000 students. Notice that a locker "change" corresponds to a divisor of the locker number. An odd number of "changes" is required to leave a locker open. Which kinds of numbers have an odd number of divisors? Only the perfect squares!

In summary, this problem has embedded in it several basic mathe-

PROBLEM The Greens are having a party. The first time the doorbell rings, 1 guest enters. On the second ring, 3 guests enter. On the third ring, 5 guests enter, and so on. That is, on each successive ring, the entering group is 2 guests larger than the preceding group. How many guests will enter on the fifteenth ring? How many guests will be present after the fifteenth ring?

Discussion Again, let's make a table and search for a pattern.

Ring number	People enter	Total present
1	1	1
2	3	4
3	5	9
4	7	16
5	9	25
6	11	36
.	.	.
.	.	.
.	.	.
n	$(2n - 1)$	n^2

This means that on the fifteenth ring, $(2 \cdot 15 - 1)$ or 29 people will enter; a total of 225 people will have arrived after the fifteenth ring.

Notice that this problem illustrates the generalization that the sum of the first n odd intergers is n^2.

PROBLEM There are 8 people in a room. Each person shakes hands with each of the other people once and only once. How many handshakes are there?

Discussion This problem yields Figure 1-3, a geometric model of a convex octagon, where the vertices represent the people and the edges and diagonals represent the handshakes (only representative handshakes shown). Thus we are asking students to identify the number of diagonals plus the number of sides of a convex polygon. The answer is given by the mathematical formula

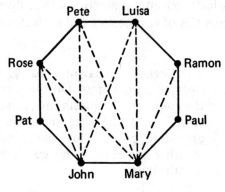

Figure 1-3

$$d = \frac{n(n-3)}{2} + n$$

This problem also illustrates the Fundamental Counting Principle. For elementary students, the problem should actually be acted out in the classroom.

2. The problem can be generalized or extended to a variety of situations.

A problem is not necessarily finished when a satisfactory solution has been found. The solution should suggest variations on parts of the original problem. The problem might be changed from a two-dimensional, plane-geometry problem to a three-space situation. Circles become spheres; rectangles become "boxes."

We should extend the problem by asking "What If . . ." questions. What if we hold one variable constant and let another change? What if the shapes of the given figures vary? What if the dimensions change? We must generalize the problem from the specific case under scrutiny to a more general case.

PROBLEM   How many squares are there on a standard checkerboard?

Discussion   This problem may be approached by considering the number of 1 X 1 squares, the number of 2 X 2 squares, the number of 3 X 3 squares, and so on up to the number of 8 X 8 squares. In tabular form these would be

Size of square	Number of squares
1 X 1	64
2 X 2	49
3 X 3	36
4 X 4	25
5 X 5	16
6 X 6	9
7 X 7	4
8 X 8	1
	Total: 204

We now generalize this problem. What if the checkerboard were 4 X 4? What if it were 5 X 5? What if it were n X n? What if it were a rectangular checkerboard with dimensions m X n?

PROBLEM   Into how many different plane regions do n lines, no three of which are concurrent and none of which are parallel, separate the plane?

Discussion   This problem can be increased to three dimensions: "Into how many different space regions do n planes that do not intersect in a line and that are not parallel separate the space?"

We can also reduce the problem to one dimension: "Into how many different linear regions do n different points in a line separate the line?"

PROBLEM   In the "equation" $(he)^2 = she$, the letters represent digits and the configurations represent numerals in base 10. Find replacements for the letters that make the statement true.

Discussion   If we were to select numerical values for s, h, and e at random, we would have approximately 1,000 possible combinations to test. However, we can impose some conditions about numbers and thus reduce our sample space radically:

1. e^2 will produce the same units digit as does e.
   ∴ e must equal 0, 1, 5, or 6.
2. $(he)^2$ will yield a three-digit number.
   ∴ $(he)^2$ must lie between 100 and 1,000, or (he) must lie between 10 and 32.

11

Now we have reduced the possibilities to only 10. However, there is a third condition:

3. *(he)* appears on both sides of the equation, in both numerals.

Testing this condition yields the unique solution $(25)^2 = 625$.

PROBLEM   Find all rectangles with integral sides whose area and perimeter are numerically equal.

Discussion   For the elementary student, we might begin by making a list of possible rectangles:

Rectangular	Perimeter	Area
3 X 2	10	6
3 X 4	14	12
3 X 5	16	15
3 X 6	18	18

To extend the problem, we now consider special rectangles, namely, squares.

Discussion   Using the diagram in Figure 1–4, we express the problem algebraically.

Figure 1–4

$$2a + 2b = ab$$

or

$$\frac{a+b}{ab} = \frac{1}{2}$$

A first solution is the 4 X 4 rectangle (square) whose perimeter and whose area both are 16. However, another set of values that satisfies the expressions is $a = 6$ and $b = 3$. This rectangle has a perimeter and an area of 18. These are the only two solutions to this problem unless we consider the degenerate case, namely the 0 by 0 rectangle.

In the previous problem, we saw that the equation we wanted to solve was

$$\frac{a+b}{ab} = \frac{1}{2}$$

This same general equation can occur in variations of the problem, as seen below.

PROBLEM   Find those pairs of integers that have 4 as their harmonic mean. (Note: The harnonic mean of two numbers is the reciprocal of the arithmetic mean of their reciprocals.)

Discussion   If we represent these integers by m and n, we obtain the relationship

$$\frac{\frac{1}{m} + \frac{1}{n}}{2} = \frac{1}{4}$$

$$\frac{1}{m} + \frac{1}{n} = \frac{1}{2}$$

$$\frac{m+n}{mn} = \frac{1}{2}$$

PROBLEM   The bus from Philadelphia to New York averages 40 miles per hour. On its return trip from New York to Philadelphia it averages 60 miles per hour. What is its average speed for the entire round trip?

Discussion   The average speed for the round trip is represented by the equation

$$\frac{\frac{1}{40} + \frac{1}{60}}{2} = \frac{1}{n}$$

where n = the average rate.

PROBLEM   The product of two integers is positive and equals twice the sum of the integers. Find the pair of integers.

13

Discussion Represent the pair of integers by r and s. Then

$$rs = 2(r + s)$$

$$1 = \frac{2(r + s)}{rs}$$

$$\frac{1}{2} = \frac{r + s}{rs}$$

These variations, which lead to the same general equation, are only one kind of problem extension. Still another kind of extension leads to further development of the original problem, as in the following case.

PROBLEM For which positive integers a, b, and c will $\frac{1}{a} + \frac{1}{b} + \frac{1}{c} = 1$?

Discussion An immediate solution is to let a, b, and c each equal 3. This yields the solution $1/3 + 1/3 + 1/3 = 1$. There is nothing in the statement of the original problem to preclude this. But while this solution does satisfy the problem, it clearly leaves us looking for more. A natural extension, then, is to add the condition that $a \neq b \neq c$. Now a solution is $a = 2, b = 3, c = 6$, since $1/2 + 1/3 + 1/6 = 1$.

A further extension might be to ask students for which positive integer n can we express n as the sum of the reciprocals of some number of different positive integers.

3. The problem lends itself to a variety of solutions.*

A problem can often be solved in many different ways. The problem-solving process may culminate in an algebraic solution, a geometric solution, or even a solution found through logical reasoning. It is of more value to the problem-solving process to solve one problem in four ways than to solve four problems, each in one way.

PROBLEM Prove: If a point lies on one side of a triangle and is equally distant from the three vertices, then the triangle is a right triangle.

Discussion 1 Let P be the point on side AB of triangle ABC such that $AP = BP = CP$. Then label the angle measures x and y, using the properties of isosceles triangles APC and BPC. (See Figure 1-5.)

---

*This section was suggested by a paper by Dr. John F. Lucas, University of Wisconsin-Oshkosh, presented at the Ninth Annual Mathematics Symposium, Frostburg State College, Frostburg, Maryland, on April 28, 1978.

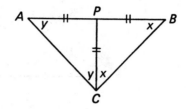

Figure 1-5

Now, since the sum of the measures of the angles of the triangle ABC equals 180°,

$$2x + 2y = 180$$
$$x + y = 90$$

which is the required proof.

Discussion 2 Triangle ABC can be inscribed in a circle, as in Figure 1-6. Since point P is equidistant from A, B, and C, then P must be the center of the circle.

Figure 1-6

This makes APB a diameter of the circle, and an angle inscribed in a semicircle is a right angle.

Discussion 3 Extend segment CP its own length along ray CP to point D. Draw DA and DB. (See Figure 1-7.)

Now consider quadrilateral $CADB$. Since its diagonals bisect each other ($CP = PD$ by construction, $AP = PB$ by the given conditions), the quadrilateral must be a parallelogram. Furthermore, since the diagonals are congruent ($APB = DPC$), the parallelogram must be a rectangle. Hence angle C is a right angle.

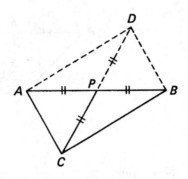

Figure 1-7

PROBLEM A farmer has some pigs and some chickens. He finds that together they have 70 heads and 200 legs. How many pigs and how many chickens does he have?

Discussion 1 The problem can be solved algebraically by using two equations in two variables:

$$1p + 1c = \;\;\;70 \text{ (heads)}$$
$$4p + 2c = 200 \text{ (legs)}$$
$$p = \;\;'30$$
$$c = \;\;\;40$$

Discussion 2 A series of successive approximations will also enable students to find the solution:

CHICKENS		PIGS		TOTAL		
Number of heads	Number of legs	Number of heads	Number of legs	Number of heads	Number of legs	
70	140	0	0	70	140	(Not enough legs)
50	100	20	80	70	180	(Still not enough legs)
40	80	30	120	70	200	

30 pigs and 40 chickens   200 legs

Discussion 3 Use the idea of a one-to-one correspondence. All chickens stand on one leg, all pigs stand on hind legs. Thus the farmer will see 70 heads and 100 legs. The extra 30 legs must belong to the pigs, since the chickens have one leg per head. Thus there are 30 pigs and 40 chickens.

WHAT MAKES A GOOD TEACHER OF PROBLEM SOLVING?

All we have said about problems, problem solving, and problem solvers depends upon the teacher for implementation and fruition. Without an interested, energetic, enthusiastic, and involved guide or model, nothing positive will take place.

Success in problem solving requires a positive teacher attitude toward the problem-solving process itself. This means that teachers must prepare carefully for problem solving, and be aware of the opportunities for problem solving that present themselves in everyday classroom situations. You may have to modify a problem to assure its pedagogical value—its scope may have to be reduced, or the problem restated in terms of the students' experiences. Knowing your students helps you make these choices. Problems should be solved in class carefully, with the teacher allowing for and encouraging a wide variety of approaches, ideas, questions, solutions, and discussions. Teachers must be confident in class, and must exhibit the same enthusiasm for the problem-solving process that they wish to instill in their students.

Some teachers dislike problem solving because they have not had enough successful experiences in this area. Practice will provide these experiences. Teachers who encourage their students to solve problems, who make the students think, and who ask carefully worded questions (rather than merely giving answers) will provide their students with a rich problem-solving experience.

CHAPTER TWO

A Workable Set of Heuristics

WHAT ARE HEURISTICS?

Problem solving is a *process*! A process that starts when the initial encounter with the problem is made and ends when the obtained answer is reviewed in light of the given information. Children must learn this *process* if they are to deal successfully with the problems they will meet in school and elsewhere. This process is complex and difficult to learn. It consists of a series of tasks and thought processes that are loosely linked together to form what is called a *set of heuristics* or a *heuristic pattern*. They are a set of suggestions and questions that a person must follow and ask themselves in order to resolve a dilemma.

Heuristics should not be confused with algorithms. Algorithms are schemas that are applied to single-class problems. In computer language, they are programs that can be called up to solve specific problems or classes of problems for which they were developed. For each problem or class of problems, there is a specific algorithm. If one chooses and properly applies the appropriate algorithms, and makes no arithmetic or mechanical errors, then the answer that is obtained will be correct. In contrast, heuristics are general and are applicable to all classes of problems. They provide the direction needed by all people to approach, understand, and obtain answers to problems that confront them.

There is no single set of heuristics for problem solving. Several people have put forth workable models, and whether the student follows the one put forth by Polya or the one that appears in this book is not important; what is important is that students learn some set of carefully developed heuristics, and that they develop the habit of applying these heuristics in all problem-solving situations.

It is apparent that simply providing students with a set of heuristics to follow would be of little value. There is quite a difference between understanding a strategy on an intellectual plane (recognizing and describing it) and being able to actually apply the strategy. Thus we must do more than merely hand the heuristics to the students— rather, instruction must focus on the thinking that the problem solver goes through as he or she considers a problem. It is the process—not the answer—that is problem solving.

Applying heuristics is a difficult skill in itself. We must spend time showing students how (and when) to use each of the heuristics—a prescriptive approach rather than merely a descriptive one. Then we must constantly use and refer to the heuristics as our students solve problems.

A SET OF HEURISTICS TO USE

Over the years, several sets of heuristics have been developed to assist students in problem solving. In the main, they are quite similar. We now put forth a set of heuristics that has proven to be successful with students and teachers at all levels of instruction:

1. Read
2. Explore
3. Select a strategy
4. Solve
5. Review and extend

These represent a continuum of thought which every person should use when confronted by a problem-solving situation. As a continuum, these are not discrete. In fact, "Read" and "Explore" could easily be considered at the same time under a single heading such as "Think." As the problem solver is exploring, he or she is considering what strategy to select.

1. Read.

1a. Note the key words.
1b. Describe the problem setting and visualize the action.
1c. Restate the problem in your own words.
1d. What is being asked for?
1e. What information is given?

PROBLEM   What is the lowest common denominator for the two fractions 1/3 and 1/12?

Discussion   Notice that the key word here is "lowest." We could find *a* common denominator easily enough by multiplying 12 × 3 to get 36. But that is not the lowest common denominator.

PROBLEM   Jeff weighs 160 pounds. His sister Nancy weighs 108 pounds. Scott weighs 26 pounds more than Nancy. What is the average weight of all three people?

Discussion   Here the key words are "more than" and "average." Words such as "more than," "less than," "subtracted from," etc., are often overlooked by students.

PROBLEM   Lucy leaves school for her home at 3:00. Thirty minutes later her sister, Carla, leaves school and overtakes Lucy at 4:00. If Carla travels at 10 miles per hour on her bike, how far from school did she catch up to Lucy?

Discussion   Can you visualize the action? Can you describe what is taking place? The key word here is "overtake."

2. Explore.

2a. Organize the information.
2b. Is there enough information?
2c. Is there too much information?
2d. Draw a diagram or construct a model.
2e. Make a chart or a table.

PROBLEM

A log is cut into 4 pieces in 12 seconds. At the same rate, how long would it take to cut the log into 5 pieces?

Discussion

Notice the key phrase "at the same rate."

In many cases, students react to this problem as an exercise in proportion:

$$\frac{4}{12} = \frac{5}{x}$$

They should draw a diagram, as in Figure 2-1. They will quickly see that the solution process should focus on the number of cuts needed to get the required number of pieces, rather than on the actual number of pieces.

Figure 2-1

Once the diagram has been interpreted, students should realize that they do not need proportions. They see that 3 cuts produced 4 pieces, and thus they need 4 cuts to produce 5 pieces. Since 3 cuts were made in 12 seconds, each cut required 4 seconds. Therefore the necessary 4 cuts will require 16 seconds.

PROBLEM

A farmer wishes to purchase a piece of land that is adjacent to his farm. The real estate agent tells him that the plot is triangular in shape, with sides of 20, 75, and 45 meters. This land will cost only $5.58 a square meter. How much should the farmer pay for the piece of land?

Discussion

The problem can be solved in a geometry class by using Heron's formula,

$$A = \sqrt{s(s-a)(s-b)(s-c)}$$

(where *s* equals half the perimeter). When the students draw a diagram, however, as in Figure 2-2, it becomes readily apparent that there is no such triangle, since the sum of two of the sides is not greater than the third side $[(45 + 20) < 75]$.

Figure 2-2

PROBLEM   Claire drove from Philadelphia to Brooklyn, then to Manhattan, then to Scarsdale. She returned over the same route. From Philadelphia to Brooklyn is 93 miles. From Brooklyn to Manhattan is 11 miles. The trip from Scarsdale to Philadelphia was 131 miles. What is the distance between Manhattan and Scarsdale?

Discussion   While the problem sounds cumbersome, confusing, and full of excess data, it is simplified by the use of a diagram, as in Figure 2-3.

Figure 2-3

$$
\begin{array}{ll}
\text{Philadelphia to Brooklyn} = & 93 \\
\text{Brooklyn to Manhattan} \;\; = & 11 \\
\underline{\text{Manhattan to Scarsdale} \;\;\; = \;\;\;\; x} \\
\qquad\qquad 131 \qquad\qquad = 104 + x
\end{array}
$$

PROBLEM   Jan has 7 rabbits. Together they eat 2 heads of lettuce each week. How many heads of lettuce will the rabbits eat in one year (52 weeks)?

Discussion   This problem contains excess information. The number of rabbits (7) is not needed to solve the problem. Yet it serves as a distractor to many students who multiply 7 X 2 X 52 and get 728 as their answer, rather than 104.

PROBLEM   The Sandwich Shop serves pizza at 85¢ a slice, ice cream cones for 75¢, and soft drinks for 60¢. Jesse bought a slice of pizza and a soft drink. How much change did he receive?

Discussion   This problem contains excess information and, at the same time, has insufficient data. The cost of the ice cream is excess, while the answer cannot be found because the amount of money given to the cashier is not known.

PROBLEM   Find the next three numbers in the sequence 2, 3, 5, 8, 12.

Discussion   We record these numbers in a row as in Figure 2-4, and examine the differences between successive terms.

Figure 2-4

The natural numbers give the first differences, and we can find the next three terms (17, 23, 30) quite easily. (There are other ways to examine this sequence. See Problem 10 in Section B.)

PROBLEM   Into how many segments do n points divide a given line segment?

Discussion   First draw a diagram, as in Figure 2-5.

Figure 2-5

Then organize the data by completing a table. Look for a pattern.

Number of points	1	2	3	4	·	·	·	n
Number of segments	2	3	4	5	·	·	·	$(n+1)$

25

3. Select a strategy.

3a. Pattern recognition
3b. Working backwards
3c. Guess and test
3d. Simulation or experimentation
3e. Reduction/solve a simpler problem
3f. Organized listing/exhaustive listing
3g. Logical deduction
3h. Divide and conquer

PROBLEM   The sides of a rectangle are 60 and 144. How long is the diagonal of the rectangle?

Discussion   The problem suggests the use of the Pythagorean Theorem. However, the numbers are extremely large. A simpler problem would be a problem with smaller numbers. In this case, we can examine a rectangle similar to the original with each linear dimension divided by 12. (See Figure 2–6.)

Figure 2–6

Now, some students may recognize the familiar 5-12-13 right triangle. Others may apply the Pythagorean Theorem:

$$5^2 + 12^2 = y^2$$
$$25^2 + 144 = y^2$$
$$169 = y^2$$
$$13 = y$$

To solve the original problem we need only multiply by the factor 12. We find that $x = 156$.

The following problem can be solved through the use of a simpler problem that is a model of the original problem but contains fewer cases.

PROBLEM   A Polaris Commuter has seats for 108 passengers. On a flight to Memphis, there was 1 empty seat for every 2 passengers actually on board. How many passengers were on the flight?

Discussion A simpler problem would be one that considered a plane with seats for 12 passengers.

E X X

E X X

E X X

E X X

Empty	People	Total
1	2	3
2	4	6
3	6	9
4	8	12

The pattern revealed by the table leads to

$$x + 2x = 108$$

PROBLEM How many different ways can you add four odd natural numbers and get 10 as the sum?

Discussion Students should remember that "sum" implies addition. They should note that they are to add four numbers, none of which can be even. This problem is an excellent illustration of the use of the guess and test strategy.

Students will try different sets of numbers to see if they add up to 10. Keep guessing and checking until all the ways have been found. Keeping the results in an organized table will help. Notice that $7 + 1 + 1 + 1$ is the same as $1 + 1 + 1 + 7$ is the same as $1 + 7 + 1 + 1$ and so on. These all count as one way.

PROBLEM There are three natural numbers that are less than one thousand which are both perfect squares and perfect cubes. Find these three numbers.

Discussion In this problem, it is particularly important that the students understand the question and the given information. The key words, "natural numbers" exclude 0 as a solution. They might even be able to guess the first two numbers that satisfy the given conditions, namely, 1 and 64. They should then make an exhaustive list of all the numbers less than 1000 that are perfect squares, and a similar list of those that are perfect cubes. They then examine the lists to find the numbers that appear on both. Preparing the lists provides an excellent opportunity to use the hand-held calculator. (The third number is 729.)

PROBLEM   On a table there are three boxes of lima beans. The boxes are labeled *A*, *B*, and *C*. The sum of the numbers of lima beans in *A* and *B* is 195. The difference between the numbers of lima beans in *B* and *C* is 150. The sum of the numbers of beans in *A* and *C* is 345. The difference between the numbers of beans in *A* and *C* is 25. How many lima beans are there in each box?

Discussion   Students should notice that the last two sentences refer to the number of lima beans in both *A* and *C*. Using this information, students might make a guess as to the correct answers. They should then check their guesses. If these guesses do not work, other guesses should be made and checked. (*A* contains 185 beans; *B* contains 10 beans; *C* contains 160 beans. Or *A* contains 160 beans; *B* contains 35 beans; *C* contains 185 beans.)

4. Solve.

4a. Carry through your strategy
4b. Use computational skills
4c. Use geometric skills
4d. Use algebraic skills
4e. Use elementary logic

Once the problem has been understood and a strategy has been selected, the student should perform the mathematics necessary to arrive at an answer.

The "answer" is not the "solution." We maintain that the solution is the process by which the answer is obtained.

PROBLEM   A basketball player can dribble a ball 18 times in 10 seconds; how many dribbles can she do in 1 minute? How long does it take to do 63 dribbles?

Discussion   Students construct a table as part of the solution to this problem. Some students may make a table that only carries the problem out through 30 seconds; others will carry the table all the way out to 60 seconds.

Seconds	10	20	30	40	50	60
Dribbles	18	36	54	72	90	108

It is interesting to note that the problem does not state that the rate is constant. Some students may wish to discuss the fact that, as time passes, the ballplayer might become tired and do fewer dribbles in each time period.

Some simple interpolation is required to find the answer to the second part of the problem. Use a proportion.

5. Review and extend.

5a. Verify your answer.
5b. Look for interesting variations on the original problem.
5c. Ask "What if . . ." questions.
5d. Discuss the solution.

PROBLEM   Find the length of 1 school desk if the sum of the lengths of 4 such desks is 56 feet.

Discussion   Notice that in this problem the word "sum" does not ensure that the problem will be solved by addition.

$$4x = 56$$

$$x = 14$$

The answer appears to be 14 feet. Are the units correct? Does the method appear to yield a correct answer? Does the answer "make sense"? (After all, 14 feet is rather a large desk.) Why or why not?

PROBLEM   How many different ways can you add four odd natural numbers and get 10 as a sum?

Discussion   We discussed this problem in a previous section. However, it lends itself to an interesting variation and extension. What if we use the set of integers in place of the natural numbers? Now, the number of answers becomes infinite. Why is this so? This should be discussed carefully.

PROBLEM   Figure 2–7 is an array of 17 toothpicks forming 6 squares. By removing exactly 6 of the toothpicks, leave exactly 2 squares.

Figure 2-7

Discussion After the thought that "It can't be done!" the initial student reaction is to think in terms of squares of the same size. With this restriction, they are right—it can't be done. However, if we are not restricted to squares of the same size (and nothing in the problem tells us we are so restricted), a solution is as depicted in Figure 2-8.

Figure 2-8

Notice that these "restrictions" are usually something that is self-imposed. As a variation of this kind of problem, an extension that students find interesting, you might try the following one.

PROBLEM Jeff and Barbara are both good chess players. They have completed 5 games, and each has won the same number of games. There were no ties. How might this have been done?

Discussion Again, the same kind of self-imposed restriction leads students to think that the two players, Barbara and Jeff, played *against each other*. Yet there is no such restriction. The problem is easily solved if we remove this self-imposed restriction and realize that they played their 5 games against different opponents.

PROBLEM Mark has accepted a new job with an unusual pay scale. He will receive $1 the first week, $2 the second week, $4 the third week, and so on. Each week the salary will be twice that of the previous week. How much money will Mark have earned after 4 weeks? After 8 weeks? After 20 weeks?

Discussion We can solve this problem by considering what happens at the end of 1 week, 2 weeks, 3 weeks, etc., and arranging the data in tabular form.

Week	Weekly salary	Total earned
1	$1	$1
2	$2	$3 (1 + 2)
3	$4	$7 (1 + 2 + 4)
4	$8	$15 (1 + 2 + 4 + 8)

Notice that the weekly salary can be expressed as a power of 2, namely $2^{(n-1)}$. The total salary can be expressed in either of two ways:

$$2^0 + 2^1 + 2^2 + 2^3 + 2^4 + \ldots + 2^{(n-1)}$$

or

$$2^n - 1$$

Thus the amount Mark earns after 4 weeks will be $2^4 - 1$, or \$15. The amount earned after 8 weeks will be $2^8 - 1$, or \$255. For the twentieth week, the amount will be $2^{20} - 1$, or \$1,048,575.

The following problem is an interesting variation of this problem involving rapid increases through the doubling process.

PROBLEM   Take a sheet of paper and tear it in half. Place the 2 pieces of paper atop one another, and tear them in half. This gives 4 pieces of paper. Place them on top of one another, and tear them in half again. Imagine continuing this process through 20 such tears. How many sheets are now in the pile of paper? If each sheet of paper is .001 inches thick, how high is the pile of paper?

Discussion   After 1 tear, the pile is 2 layers thick. After 2 tears, it is 4 layers thick. After n such tears, the pile will be 2^n layers thick. After 20 such tears, the pile will be 2^{20} or 1,048,576 layers thick. If the paper has a thickness of .001 inches, the pile will be about 87 feet (or 1,048 inches) high.

APPLYING THE HEURISTICS

Now that the heuristic model has been developed, let's apply it to several problems. As the solutions are developed, be sure that you are aware of the thought processes being utilized in each step. Remember, problem solving is a process. The answer is merely the final outcome.

PROBLEM   Twelve couples have been invited to a party. The couples will be seated at a series of small square tables that can seat one person on each side. The tables are placed end to end so as to form one large long table. How many of these small tables are needed to seat all 24 people?

Discussion

1. Read.

Note key words. Describe the problem setting and visualize the action. Restate the problem. What is being asked for? What facts are given?

The key words in the problem are "square tables," "twelve couples," and "placed end to end." We must find the number of tables required. Notice that 12 couples translates to 24 people.

2. Explore.

Draw a diagram.

Draw a picture of what the situation looks like for 1 table, for 2 tables, for 3 tables, etc. (See Figure 2–9.)

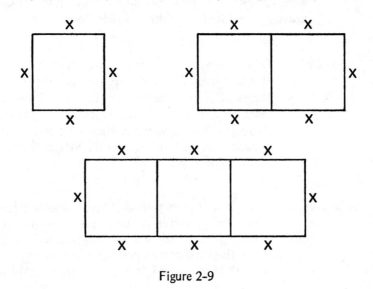

Figure 2–9

Make a table. Record the data. Look for patterns.

Number of tables	1	2	3	4	•	•	•	n
Number of guests	4	6	8	10	•	•	•	24

There seems to be a pattern here. As we add a table, the number of guests that can be seated is increased by 2.

3. Select a strategy.

Look for a simpler problem.

Suppose we limit the number of guests to a smaller number, say 16. Let's see if our pattern holds true. Extend the table.

Number of tables	1	2	3	4	5	6	7
Number of guests	4	6	8	10	12	14	16

Conjecture. Form a tentative hypothesis.

Since the pattern seems to be holding true for 16 guests, we can continue to add 1 table for every 2 additional guests until we reach our required number of 24 guests. We thus add 4 additional tables for the additional guests (16 + 8 = 24). This is our hypothesis: it will take 11 tables to accommodate 24 guests.

4. Solve.

Carry through your strategy.

The answer is obtained by continuing the table until we reach the required number of guests.

Number of tables	1	2	3	4	5	6	7	8	9	10	11
Number of guests	4	6	8	10	12	14	16	18	20	22	24

It will take 11 tables to seat 24 guests.

5. Review and extend.

Verify your answer. Look for variations. Ask "What if . . ." questions. Describe the solution.

Verify your answer by selecting a different strategy, namely simulation or experimentation. Place 11 small squares (to represent the tables) in a row, end to end. Count the places to be certain that the tables actually seat the 24 guests.

We might ask our students to develop a formula for seating any given number of guests *n*. This yields the expression

$$t = \frac{n-2}{2}$$

where *t* represents the number of tables.

Or we might ask for a formula to determine how many guests we can seat, given the number of tables.

$$n = 2t + 2$$

or

$$n = 2(t + 1)$$

Several "What if . . . ?" questions should be asked:

(a) What if two people could be seated at each side of the table?
(b) What if the tables were placed to form a large square (either open or closed)?
(c) What if, in the formula, we consider $n = 2$ or $n =$ an odd number?

PROBLEM   Jan and Louis are making a square design out of square tiles. Louis puts a red tile in the center. Jan then puts 8 green tiles around it to form a second square ring. Louis then puts 16 yellow tiles around these to form a third square ring. How many tiles will there be altogether to form a five-ring design?

Discussion   **1. Read.**

The key words are "square tiles," and "square design."

2. Explore.

Draw a diagram that simulates the action.

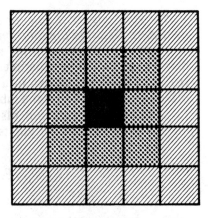

Figure 2-10

Now make a table to organize the data. Look for patterns.

Ring number	Number of tiles added	Total number of tiles
1	1	1
2	8	9
3	16	25

3. Select a strategy.

Look for a pattern. Reduction.
   By reducing the problem to its simplest case—a one-tile ring—we will observe what happens as we increase the design, ring by ring.

4. Solve.

Carry through your strategy.
   Notice that the total number of tiles appears to be the square of the odd numbers. Let's continue the table:

Ring number	Number of tiles added	Total number of tiles
1	1	1
2	8	9
3	16	25
4	24	49
5	32	81

There will be 81 tiles in the fifth ring.

5. Review and extend.

(a) How many tiles are being added in each ring?
(b) Can you develop a formula for the number of tiles being added in each ring?
(c) Can you develop a formula for the total number of tiles in the figure at the end of each ring?
(d) Beginning with the third ring, let us remove the innermost ring at the same time that we add a new outer ring. This leaves us only three rings in the figure at any given time. What is the formula that will reveal the number of tiles in the figure at any time?

$$[T = 16n - 24 \text{ or}$$
$$T = (2n - 1)^2 - (2n - 5)^2]$$

35

CHAPTER THREE

The Pedagogy of Problem Solving

Problem solving is a process. Thus we must develop a set of heuristics to follow and then be certain to use it! Whether we use the heuristics developed in Chapter 2, the four-step heuristics of Polya, or some other set of seven, eight, or even more steps is not important. What is important is that students learn a heuristic model, develop an organized set of "questions" to ask themselves, and then constantly refer to them when confronted by a problem situation.

What can the teacher do to assist students in achieving this important goal? In this chapter we will present methods that the teacher can employ in the classroom to assist students in the utilization of heuristics in their development of problem-solving skills. Activities are included for use with students.

1. Create an atmosphere of success.

The old adage "Nothing succeeds like success" holds true in the mathematics classroom. Remember: if a student refuses to even attempt to solve a problem, there can be no problem-solving activity. Choose the problems carefully. Begin with relatively simple problems so as to ensure a reasonable degree of success. If students are successful, they are likely to be "turned on" to problem solving, whereas repeated failure or constant frustration can have a devastating effect on motivation, attitude, and the desire to continue. However, remember that success must be truly earned, not just "given."

The breadth and depth of knowledge required, as well as the sequence of problems chosen, should be kept in mind as major criteria for developing suitable problem-solving situations. Consider the possibility of a series of brief, quickly done problems, each one leading to a more difficult problem, until the original problem-solving task has been completed. This procedure of breaking up a problem into a series of short steps will help those students with short attention spans to enjoy success and to become interested in progress toward the solution of problems.

PROBLEM   In a class, half of the students are boys. Six boys are present. One-fourth of the boys are present. How many students (boys and girls) are there in the entire class, when all students are present?

Discussion   Introduction of this problem might be followed by a series of brief questions. For instance:

1. How many boys are present?
2. If this is one-fourth of the boys on roll, how many boys are on roll?
3. What part of the whole class is boys?

Answering these short questions could easily lead the student to the solution of the original problem, namely 48 students.

Success means more than the correct answer. Becoming absorbed in a problem and making a sustained attempt at solution is also success.

2. Encourage your students to solve problems.

In order for students to become good problem solvers, they must be constantly exposed to and involved in problem solving. In teaching someone to swim, the "theory" can go just so far; eventually, the real ability to swim must come from actually swimming. It is the same way in problem solving. Students must solve problems! The teacher should try to find problems that are of interest to the students. Listen to them as they talk; they will often tell you about the things in which they are interested. (Problems derived from television and sports always generate enthusiasm among students.)

PROBLEM   The weight of a $1 bill is 1 gram. A basketball player's salary is $1 million. The player insists on being paid in $1 bills. Could the player carry his salary in a suitcase? Suppose he decided to accept $20 bills instead?

Discussion   Consider that the example concerns itself not only with weight, but also with volume (of the suitcase). Yet no dimensions have been given. ($1,000,000 = 1,000,000 grams = 1 metric ton.)

PROBLEM   Superman and Lothar are mortal enemies. Superman is about to enter Lothar's secret hideaway. Inside, Lothar has 5 "zap" guns, each of which can fire 3 kryptonite bullets at Superman. How many times can Lothar fire a kryptonite bullet at Superman?

Discussion   Notice the similarity to the basic textbook problem "Jane wants to buy 3 oranges at 5¢ each. How much money does she need to buy the oranges?"

ACTIVITY   Take several exercises from the students' textbook. Encourage the students to change the setting of the problem to one that is more interesting to them. Emphasize that the problem must contain the same data as the original.

Discussion   One effect of this activity will be to force the students to decide what the problem is really all about. At the same time, they will be engaged in creating problems similar to the original but more interesting to them.

Another way to encourage your students to solve problems is to stop occasionally in class in order to analyze what it is that you are doing and why the processes were undertaken in a particular manner. Focus the students' attention on the larger issue of a general strategy as well as on the specific details of the particular problem at hand. If difficulties arise, make yourself available to *help* students; do not solve the problem for them.

ACTIVITY Present students with problems that do not contain specific numbers. Ask them to discuss what operations are called for.
EXAMPLE: Jeff wants to buy a pen, a notebook, and an eraser for school. How can he be sure that he has sufficient money?
EXAMPLE: You know the age of an elephant in years and months. How many months old is the elephant?

Try to solve problems in more than one way. Doing this will increase the number of alternative approaches available to the students the next time they face a problem situation.

PROBLEM A, B, and C decide to play a game of cards. They agree on the following procedure: When a player loses a game, he or she will double the amount of money that each of the other players already has. First A loses a hand and doubles the amount of money that B and C each have. Then B loses a hand and doubles the amount of money that A and C each have. Then C loses a hand and doubles the amount of money that A and B each have. The three players then decide to quit, and they find that each player now has $8. Who was the biggest loser?

Discussion This problem can be solved in an algebra class by writing a series of 3 equations in 3 unknowns. Once this is done, the system of equations can be solved easily.
An alternative approach might be to suggest to the class that they try to solve the problem by working backwards. This quickly yields the solution, and at an artistic, less mathematically sophisticated level. At the same time, it provides the students with an additional approach to problem solving (namely, working backwards).

| | Player | | |
A	B	C	
8	8	8	game 3
4	4	16	game 2
2	14	8	game 1
13	7	4	start

3. Teach students how to read the problem.

Fundamental to any problem solving is understanding the situation. In most cases, this implies the ability to read with understanding. Students often overlook essential ideas and implications within the context of the problem. Since most problems in school are presented in written form, proper reading habits are essential.

ACTIVITY

It is important to alert your students to the fact that not all mathematics is read from left to right. The eye views simple expressions such as

$$\frac{3}{8} + \frac{4}{8} = \frac{7}{8}$$

in a variety of different directions, as shown by the following "arrow diagram":

Prepare a transparency containing several different mathematical expressions. Have students draw correct arrow diagrams for each one.

Many activities should be used to help students sharpen their ability to read critically and carefully for meaning. One such technique is to have the students underline or circle words that they consider to be key words in a problem. Discuss these words with the class. Have students indicate why they consider these particular words to be key words.

PROBLEM

If the length of the Loch Ness monster is 20 meters and half of its own length, how long is the monster?

42

Discussion   Some students will decide that the monster is 20 meters long plus half of 20 meters (10), or a total of 30 meters in length. These students have overlooked the words "and half of its own length." Once these words have been carefully considered, students should interpret the problem to mean that the monster's full length is the sum of 20 meters and half the total length. Thus the monster is really divided into two equal halves. If the monster's full length is one of these halves plus 20 meters, then the 20 meters must represent the other half, and the full length of the monster is 40 meters. The same result can easily be found with the algebraic equation

$$x = 20 + \frac{x}{2}$$

where x is the total length of the Loch Ness monster.

ACTIVITY   Write a problem on a slip of paper. Have one student read the problem silently, put it away, and then relate the problem in his or her own words to the rest of the class. In this way, students often reveal whether they have found the facts that are really important to the solution of the problem, or whether they have missed the point entirely.

ACTIVITY   Show a problem on a transparency on the overhead projector. After a short period of time, turn the projector off and have the class restate the problem in their own words.

ACTIVITY   One way to encourage practice in reading mathematics problems slowly and for understanding is to mimeograph a page from a mathematics textbook, cut the page into pieces much like those of a jigsaw puzzle, and have the students put the page together again.

Since many words have a special meaning in the mathematics classroom which is different from the regular meaning, the class should discuss a list of such words together with their various meanings. (A beneficial project would be the compilation of a dictionary in which each word is defined mathematically and in other contexts.)

ACTIVITY   Discuss the different meanings of the following words:

volume	chord	function	prime
root	difference	mean	times
count	element	power	

ACTIVITY   Duplicate a series of problems, leaving out every tenth word. Ask your students to try to fill in the blanks. (Note: As your students become more proficient in this skill, you can leave out every seventh word, every fifth word, etc.)

After the students have gained an understanding of a problem and can relate it in their own words, they will need to be able to identify the question that must be answered and the necessary facts.

ACTIVITY   Give students a set of problems and have them circle or under-line the sentence that tells them what they must find. Note that this "question" may be in question or interrogative form or may be stated in declarative form.

1. A farmer has a field in the shape of a rectangle that is 100 feet long and 45 feet wide. Find the number of feet of fencing required to enclose the field.
2. Mary went to the supermarket and spent $6.72. How much change will she receive from a $10 bill?

The information necessary to solve a problem sometimes appears in verbal form, but other times it appears in picture form. Give the students activities similar to the ones that follow to help them determine which facts in a problem are important.

ACTIVITY   Look at the toys in Figure 3-1. Then answer the questions.

39¢

79¢

89¢

Marbles

25¢

98¢

Figure 3-1

1. Which toy costs 98¢

2. How much does the jack-in-the-box cost?
3. Which toy is the most expensive?
4. Which toy is the least expensive?
5. Which toys cost less than 50¢?
6. Which toys cost more than $1.00?

ACTIVITY   Read the following paragraph. Then answer the questions.

Mr. and Mrs. Gonzalez and their three children went to the baseball game between the Los Angeles Dodgers and the New York Mets. Tickets were $7.50 for adults and $2.50 for children. The game lasted 2½ hours and the Dodgers won, 7–5. They left the ballpark at 4:00 p.m.

1. Which teams were playing?
2. How much do adult tickets cost?
3. How long did the game last?
4. How many members of the Gonzalez family went to the game?
5. What time did the game end?
6. Where was the game played?

These last two questions should evoke some discussion, since neither of them is directly answerable. In all cases, it is important that a discussion be held with the students regarding the facts that appear in the problem as opposed to inferences which they might have made.

Reading a problem also means being able to discriminate between necessary and unnecessary information. In many cases, information is put into a problem to serve as distractors. In other cases, necessary data may have been omitted. We strongly recommend that students be given activities that will enable them to distinguish between necessary and superfluous data, as well as to determine when there is insufficient data to solve the problem. Students should supply the necessary facts when they are missing from a problem.

ACTIVITY   Give the students a problem in written form. Include a great deal of extra information. Tell the students to cross out every thing they think is unnecessary. Have them read what remains. Do they have the correct information to solve the problem? Do they still have too much?

ACTIVITY   Prepare a collection of problems on 3" X 5" cards. Some of the problems should have excess information. Others should have missing data. Students must decide which, and supply the data needed to solve the problem if the facts are missing.

45

ACTIVITY   Problem Reader-Problem Solver is an activity that helps to sharpen students' ability to read and comprehend a problem quickly and accurately. It is particularly effective in helping students ascertain the important aspects of a problem. The students in the class are paired off. One member of each pair is designated as the Problem Reader, while the other is designated as the Problem Solver. The Problem Solver closes his or her eyes, while a problem is displayed via the overhead projector, for 15 to 30 seconds. During this time, the Problem Reader may take any notes or make any drawings that he or she deems necessary. The problem is then taken off the overhead, and the Problem Readers present the problem to their partners who must solve the problem. The Problem Reader and the Problem Solver then reverse roles and play the game again.

ACTIVITY   Divide the class up into 3 or 4 teams consisting of 5–8 students on each team. Tell the students that they are going on a mathematical Scavenger Hunt. Each team must find problems in their textbook as asked for on the list of items which they will receive. Present each team with a list of questions similar to the following:

1. Find a problem where the answer is in yards.
2. Find a problem where the answer is in miles per hour.
3. Find a problem where the answer is in years.
4. Find a problem where the answer is in hours.
5. Find a problem that deals with a person's earnings.
6. Find a problem that has a setting in the sea.
7. Find a problem that deals with coins.
8. Find a problem that contains too much information.

These and similar activities available from the school's reading specialist will teach your students to read the problems more critically and to understand them better.

4. Involve your students in the problem.

Customize the problems to include your students. Their names should appear in the problems. Also, let them act out the story. Create problems which require action. Let the students experiment!

PROBLEM   How fast can you bounce a basketball? That is, how many times can you bounce the basketball in 1 minute?

PROBLEM   Can you roll a marble along the chalk tray in your classroom as quickly as you can run a distance of 100 yards?

PROBLEM   What is the sum of the ages of everyone in your class in years and months?

PROBLEM   What percent of your class was born in June?

Notice that these problems allow the students to actually get into the problem. They become a part of the story. Out come stopwatches, basketballs, marbles, and so on. The entire class becomes actively engaged in the problem-solving process.

PROBLEM   Three boys stood on a scale and put a nickel in the slot. The scale showed 390 pounds as their total weight. One boy stepped off the scale. It then showed 255 pounds. The second boy stepped off the scale, and it then showed 145 pounds. Find the weights of all three boys.

Discussion   In class, you could ask three boys to actually act out this problem. They might step back onto the "scale" to check their weights.

Using manipulable materials in problem solving is another way to enable your students to become active participants. If students must work directly with the materials to solve problems, they cannot just sit back and become spectators. The materials can easily be stored in shoeboxes or in large envelopes, along with a series of activity cards posing the problems.

PROBLEM   How many 3-rod trains can you make that are equal in length to 1 orange rod? (Cuisenaire Rods)

Discussion   Notice that this is the same problem as "How many different ways can you select 3 natural numbers such that their sum is 10?" Yet it involves the use of concrete materials.

PROBLEM   On a geoboard, use rubber bands to construct several figures with an area of 16 square units. How many can you make?

47

PROBLEM   Figure 3-2 contains pictures of 3 figures that were made with the 7 Tangram pieces. Try to make each one using all 7 pieces. Record your solution on paper. (Tangrams)

Figure 3-2

5. Require your students to create their own problems.

Nothing helps students to become better problem solvers than having them make up their own problems. In order to create a problem, students must know the anatomy of a problem. They must relate facts, questions, and distractors. We know that students create excellent problems. In fact, their problems are usually more relevant (and often more complex) than the ones typically found in textbooks.

However, in order to generate problems, students need something to write about, the setting. Presenting a suitable stimulus will aid pupils in this endeavor.

ACTIVITY   Provide students with a set of answers such as 15 books, $7.32, 8 miles, 12½ gallons, etc. Have them create problems for which each of these is the answer.

ACTIVITY   Show pictures that have been taken from old magazines, old textbooks, etc. Have the students make up their own numerical data and a story problem to fit each picture.

Discussion This activity helps students learn to decide on numerical data that makes sense, for they must use realistic numbers in their problem designing. At the same time, this activity helps students to integrate mathematical problem solving with other subjects, such as social studies, language arts, and science.

ACTIVITY Ask your students to write a "menu problem." That is, given the following menu, write a problem about it.

Hot dog	.95
Hamburger	1.25
Pizza (slice)	.85
Tuna sandwich	1.25
Grilled cheese sandwich	1.05
Apple	.25
Bananas	2 for .45
Milk (white)	.30
Milk (chocolate)	.35
Candy	2 for .65

Sharing problems that have been written by other students should be an integral part of your classroom procedure. The fact that the problems have been designed by classmates usually heightens interest in solving them. These problems may simply be variations of other problems that students have seen, or they may be entirely original creations. Remember that not all of the problems need have an answer; it is the problem-solving process that is being stressed. In fact, it is often desireable to have students create problems with too much information or insufficient information. This is an interesting and worthwhile task, for when other students attempt to solve these problems, they usually find themselves heavily involved in determining the amount of information given.

PROBLEM How many slices of pizza can four teenagers eat?

PROBLEM Find the area of a parallelogram whose adjacent sides are 8 centimeters and 6 centimeters.

PROBLEM Jan has 84 seashells in her collection. She decided to give 5 shells to each of 3 friends. How many shells did she give away?

In all cases above, the discussion of the information given in the problem is of more value than the answer.

Notice that problems that appear in textbooks often emphasize one particular skill or operation. On the other hand, student-generated problems frequently involve extraneous data and possibly more than one operation.

6. Have your students work together in pairs or small groups.

Team problem solving and group brainstorming are viable techniques in the business world. Rarely does any one person solve major problems alone. While the final decisions do fall on one person, the group input helps the problem-solving process. A student's inability or refusal to help in the group process can be a direct hindrance to decision making.

Brainstorming is not ordinarily used in the traditional classroom. Students have had no training nor experiences in sharing of ideas and the interaction required. Thus, the classroom teacher must provide guidance and practice in the particular skills involved in sharing ideas. The teacher should keep in mind that in brainstorming:

1. There should be no evaluation of any kind. People have a tendency to become defensive of their own ideas. In addition, other people may not participate if they feel that they are to be formally judged.
2. Everyone is encouraged to allow their imaginations to run rampant.
3. Participants are encouraged to put forth as many ideas as possible.
4. Everyone is encouraged to build upon the ideas or to modify the ideas of others.

The interaction provided by cooperating students will help them learn to modify one another's thinking, and to defend their own positions while considering the positions of other students. They will also learn to express their thoughts more clearly by the use of precise language, especially mathematical terminology—students will find it difficult to communicate with others unless they use language that every member of the group can agree upon.

The group may want to focus on a problem-solving situation as a series of motion-picture frames. The sequential nature of this image helps students decide what comes first, what comes second, and so on. With contributions from various members of the group, the class can develop a sequence of activities to solve the problem.

ACTIVITY   Divide your class into groups of 5 or 6 students. Each group should be provided with a trio of totally unrelated words, such as:

(a) pencil—apple—football
(b) elephant—lollypop—clock
(c) kumquat—sunglasses—flashlight
(d) basket—radio—cereal

Notice that the words in each group do not appear to have anything in common. It is the group's task to think of some link. After a few minutes, explain and discuss each group's solution to the problem.

ACTIVITY — Using the "Linking-Thinking" activity described above, assign the group the task of writing a brief story in which each of the three objects named plays an integral role.

ACTIVITY — "Notice" is a quiz that is administered to students in groups. The entire group must arrive at one single True or False decision for each statement. Here are some sample statements:

(a) The Statue of Liberty uses her right hand to hold the torch. (True)
(b) A recording on a turntable will turn clockwise. (True)
(c) Page 82 of a book is a right-side page. (False)
(d) Most pencils have eight sides. (False)
(e) Q is the only letter that is missing on a telephone. (False)

ACTIVITY — Students are divided into groups of five or six. Each group is given the task of building the highest possible "tower" out of the available materials in a fixed time period. The group must decide who will be responsible for the various activities required to build the tower. Materials might consist of the following, or variations or combinations thereof: small boxes (cereal boxes, for example), construction paper and Scotch tape, rolls from inside paper towels, pieces of styrofoam, metal scraps, etc. The only restriction is that the tower may not be attached in any way to the ceiling for support.

Problems in which students have to list all possible outcomes lend themselves well to the group discussion method. It is the group's decision as to when all outcomes have been listed.

PROBLEM — Your group has been given $1,000,000 to spend in a 24-hour period. How would you spend the money? (You may buy only one of each item you select.)

51

While we do not advocate that students solve all problems in groups, the group process is a good method for allowing students to develop a respect for one another's abilities, and to learn to look for many possibilities in solving problems.

7. Encourage the use of freehand drawings.

Drawings do help students in problem solving. However, a beginning problem solver has a tendency to "measure" to find an answer, rather than to think the problem through or to demonstrate its solution mathematically. The use of freehand drawings will discourage students from relying on their drawings for measuring the answer. This does not mean, however, that you should allow or accept sloppy, inaccurate sketches. Students should draw neat, carefully labeled diagrams. Perpendiculars should look as if they form 90° angles; equal lengths should be drawn approximately equal.

This means, too, that the teacher must serve as a model for the students. When drawing diagrams at the board, make them carefully, but without the use of tools that differ from those the students may use. While rulers should not be used, a straightedge might be allowed. Practice in making freehand drawings is essential, since few teachers are so artistically inclined that they can draw well the first few times they attempt freehand drawings.

ACTIVITY Distribute a series of problem situations that can be described by a drawing. Have each student make a drawing to illustrate the action. Discuss the various drawings they have made.

ACTIVITY Distribute several drawings that illustrate problem situations. Have your students make up a problem for which the given sketch is appropriate. Discuss these problems with the entire class.

ACTIVITY Draw various figures on several 3" x 5" cards. Spatial geometry offers many suitable drawings for this activity. Give one card to a student. Allow him or her to study the card for one minute. At the end of that time, the student must give back the card and try to replicate the drawing on the board. Then give the card back, or ask the rest of the class if they can decide what was drawn.

ACTIVITY   Prepare several transparencies of simple figures. Project these for thirty seconds to one minute, depending on the complexity of the drawing. When the projector is turned off, have each student attempt to reproduce the figure. Have each student compare his or her response with other students', and then with the original drawing.

8. Suggest alternatives when the present approach has apparently yielded all possible information.

The mind-set (preconceived idea) that many students have often leads them to a dead end. This is not unusual, nor is it unexpected. In fact, the condition is referred to as the *einstellung* effect. This is a predisposing condition or mind-set, that usually leads to the same end over and over again, by blocking out any kind of variable behavior. This mind set must be changed and some other approach undertaken if the student has not successfully resolved the problem. Many students give up, or follow the same path again and again. It is at this point that some teachers err; they often direct the students through the most efficient path to the solution, rather than allowing further exploration. The teacher should guide the additional exploration by pointing out facts and inferences that might have been overlooked.

ACTIVITY   Present a problem to the class. Have students work in groups and attempt to solve the problem in as many different ways as possible. Have each group present its solutions to the entire class. See which group can find the greatest number of solutions.

PROBLEM   In Figure 3–3, *AB* and *CD* are perpendicular diameters of length 8 centimeters, intersecting at *O*. Any point *F* is selected on arc *AC*. Perpendiculars *FG* and *FH* are drawn to *OA* and *OC*, respectively. Find the length of segment *GH*.

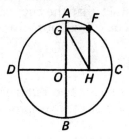

Figure 3–3

Discussion   In solving this problem, most students have a mind-set that suggests the use of the Pythagorean Theorem in triangle *GHO*. Once they have exhausted all the information in the problem, however, the teacher might suggest to them that they consider the rectangle *FGOH* and *both diagonals.*

PROBLEM   David is serving a fresh apple pie to his three brothers and himself. His older brother, Mike, bets his share that David cannot cut the pie into four equal portions without lifting his knife and/or going back over a cut. David thinks for a minute and then wins the bet. How does he do this?

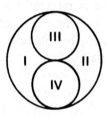

Figure 3–4

Discussion   David cuts the pie with a "figure eight" cut passing through the center of the pie, as shown in Figure 3–4.

Since the radius of the original pie is *r*, its area equals πr^2. Thus the area of each small circle (labeled III and IV) is

$$\pi \cdot \left(\frac{r}{2}\right)^2 \qquad \text{or} \qquad \pi \frac{r^2}{4}$$

which is one-fourth of the original pie. By symmetry, portions I and II are equal. Thus each piece (I, II, III, IV) is one-fourth of the original pie. Once students rid themselves of the mind-set that the cuts must be straight lines, the problem can then be solved more readily.

PROBLEM   The sum of two numbers is 7 and their product is 25. Find the sum of their reciprocals.

Discussion   The immediate reaction to this problem would be to let *x* and *y* represent the two numbers and form the two equations

$$x + y = 7$$

$$xy = 25$$

which are then solved simultaneously. As the equations are solved, we are led through the quadratic formula, which yields complex roots. In addition, students must rationalize the denominators of two expressions in the form $1/(a + bi)$ and $1/(a - bi)$.

If students have been taught to search for alternate solutions, they might work backwards. Notice that the original problem asks for the sum of the reciprocals, not the value of the two numbers. Thus we wish to find the value of $\frac{1}{x} + \frac{1}{y}$

which is $\frac{x + y}{xy}$ or $\frac{7}{25}$.

PROBLEM A pirate ship at point A in Figure 3–5 is 50 meters directly north of point C on the shore. Point D, also on the shore and due east of point C, is 130 meters from point C. Point B, a lighthouse, is due north of point D and 80 meters from point D. The pirate ship must touch the shoreline and then sail to the lighthouse. Find the location of point X on the shoreline so that the path from A to X to B will be a minimum.

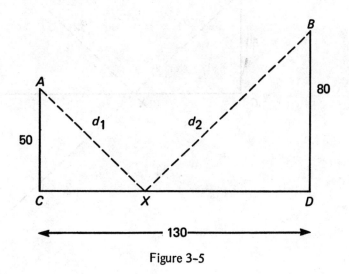

Figure 3–5

Discussion If students decide to use a calculator, they can use a series of successive approximations, as follows:

CX	XD	d_1	d_2	$d_1 + d_2$
0	130	50.0	152.6	202.6
20	110	53.9	136.0	189.9
40	90	64.0	120.4	184.44
50	80	70.7	113.1	183.8 ←(approximate
60	70	78.1	106.3	184.41 location of
80	50	94.3	94.3	188.6 X)
100	30	104.4	85.4	189.8
130	0	139.3	80.0	219.3

Although these calculations do yield an approximate location for point X, the teacher might offer the following suggestions to students to help them "exactly" locate point X. The term "minimum distance" is the same as "shortest path." Students should realize that the shortest path between two points in a plane is a straight line. Thus, if we reflect segment BD its own length to B' so that B and B' are on opposite sides of CD, we can draw AB', as in Figure 3–6.

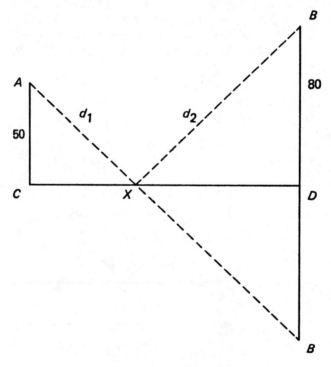

Figure 3–6

Now, since AB' is a minimum, and since triangle BDX is congruent to triangle B'DX, segment BX (or d_2) is equal to segment B'X. Thus point X is the exact location we wish.

PROBLEM   In an office there are two square windows. Each window is 4 feet high, yet one window has an area twice that of the other window. Explain how this can take place.

Discussion   The usual way to envision a square window is with the sides parallel to and perpendicular to the floor. However, if we consider a window which has been rotated through 45°, we can readily see the explanation.

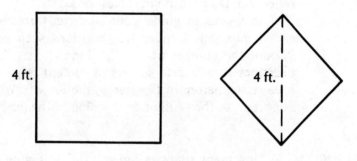

Figure 3-7

When students are stuck, you might suggest that they look back at other problems they have solved in the past that were similar to the problem under consideration. This might lead to some ideas of what to do. Even a suggestion as to what might be done at a particular point is sometimes in order. Thus you could suggest to students that "it might be a good idea" if they

1. made a guess and checked it
2. tried a simpler version of the problem
3. made a table
4. drew a diagram
5. used a physical model
6. used a calculator
7. worked backwards
8. looked for a pattern
9. divided the problem into several parts and solved each
10. used logical thinking
11. examined a similar problem.

Even encouraging students to simply pause and carefully reflect on the problem is a good technique to try when students are totally stymied.

9. Raise creative, constructive questions.

Teachers often commit an error when their students are stuck. In the interest of time, they often take the students directly to the answer by showing them a finished solution. Instead, you should ask questions that will provide the students with guidance and direction, yet will allow for a wide range of responses. Give them time to think before they respond to your questions. Research indicates that the average teacher allows only up to 3 seconds when students respond to a question. Problem solving is a complex process—you must allow time for reflection. Don't rush your questions.

In trying to guide your students through a solution, use open-ended questions frequently. Questions such as "How many . . . ?", "Count the number of . . . ", "Find all . . . ", are all nonthreatening questions that lead to successful student responses. In addition, as we have stated before in Chapter 1, the use of "What if . . . " questions is important to their full understanding of the problem.

PROBLEM   How many triangles can you find in Figure 3–8?

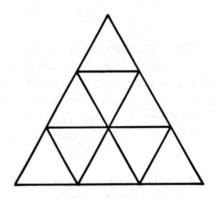

Figure 3–8

Discussion   The above question cannot be answered incorrectly, even if the student can find only a minimal number of triangles.

Throughout the problem-solving process, let your questions cause the students to reflect back on the problem solution. Too often we tend to turn away from a problem that has been "solved" (i.e., for which an answer has been found) in order to move on to the next problem. Thus we miss a chance to glean extra values from our energy. Examine the solution carefully; ask questions about key points. Ask many

"What if ... " questions. Ask students "What new question does this suggest?" or "How else might I ask this question?"

Other questions that you might ask include:

1. Do you recognize any patterns?
2. What is another way to approach the problem?
3. What kind of problem does this remind you of?
4. What would happen if ...
    the conditions of the problem were changed to ... ?
    the converse were asked?
    we imposed additional conditions?
5. What further exploration of this problem can you suggest?

Be careful that

1. Your question is not changed or altered while the students are considering it;
2. You give the students ample time before repeating the question;
3. You do not answer your own question until you are certain that the students have finished their responses. Perhaps then, an additional hint or comment might lead them in the right direction.

10. Emphasize creativity of thought and imagination.

In a positive classroom atmosphere, students can be as free-thinking as they wish. You should not penalize "way out" answers if they show some thought on the part of the students. Again, keep in mind that it is the problem-solving *process* that is important!

ACTIVITY   A student's response to the question "How can I divide 25 pieces of candy among three people?" was "I'll take 23 pieces and give 1 to each of my friends!" Discuss the answer.

ACTIVITY   Karen drove from New York to Atlanta in 16 hours, a total distance of 800 miles. How fast did she drive? Discuss this problem.

The two activities suggested above will often yield answers that are quite different from what was expected. Students can interpret what is given and what is asked for in a variety of ways. Which way may be different in meaning, yet quite appropriate in thought. In all cases, you must lead the class in a thorough discussion of *why* these various interpretations took place.

Systematic trial and error and careful, selective guessing are both creative techniques to use. (How many times have teachers been heard to say to a student, "Do you *know*, or are you just guessing?") Guessing, or careful trial and error, should be practiced and encouraged. It is difficult but important to be a good guesser.

PROBLEM   I am thinking of 2 two-digit numbers. They have the same digits, only reversed. The difference between the numbers is 54, while the sum of the digits of each number is 10. Find the 2 numbers.

Discussion   While most algebra students could complete this problem by solving a pair of linear equations in two unknowns simultaneously, creative use of trial and error makes this problem suitable for a problem-solving activity at other levels as well. The teacher might suggest the following steps:

1. List all the two-digit numbers whose digit sum is 10:

$$19, 28, 37, 46, 55, 64, 73, 82, 91$$

2. Subtract pairs with the same digits:

$$91 - 19 = 72$$
$$82 - 28 = 54$$
$$73 - 37 = 36$$
$$64 - 46 = 18$$

At this point, you might consider asking the students how they know that 82, 28 is the *only* pair of two-digit numbers that satisfies the original problem.

PROBLEM   Peggy and Barbara each want to buy a turkey for Thanksgiving. Peggy needs a larger turkey, since she has a bigger family. The butcher has two turkeys left. He tells the women that "Together they weigh a total of 20 pounds, and the smaller one costs 2¢ a pound more than the larger one." Barbara pays $3.36 for the smaller one, while Peggy pays $5.98 for the larger. How much does each weigh?

Discussion   Although the problem can be solved algebraically quite readily, let's see if we can solve the problem with systematic trial and error. Suppose we assume that the small turkey weighs, say, 8 pounds. Then the larger turkey must weigh 20 − 8 or 12 pounds. Since the bigger bird cost $5.98, the price per pound must have been 5.98/12, or almost 50¢. The smaller bird cost 2¢ per pound more, or 52¢, per pound. But only $3.36 was actually spent, and 8 × .52 ≠ 3.36.

Our next try should be a smaller weight for the smaller bird. In one or two more tries, we should arrive at the solution of 7 pounds and 13 pounds.

Puzzle problems that involve practice in arranging and rearranging numbers are helpful in developing student skills at organized guessing.

PROBLEM   Which disk in Figure 3–9 would you move to another box so that all three boxes would then have a sum of 15? Show your move.

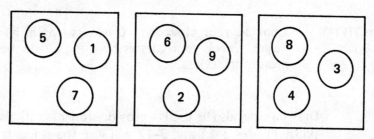

Figure 3–9

PROBLEM   Place the numbers 1, 2, 3, 4, 5, and 6 in the spaces provided in Figure 3–10 so that each side of the triangle adds up to 10.

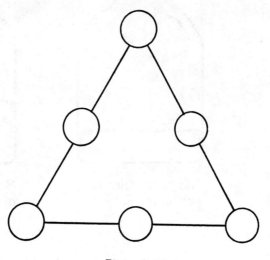

Figure 3–10

To help your students practice their guessing and estimating techniques, you might use several activities similar to the following.

ACTIVITY   Find a book with a lot of pages. Close your eyes and place a bookmark anywhere in the book. Now open your eyes and look at the bookmark. Guess the number of the page it is marking. Try this five times. Keep a record of how many times your guess was within 15 pages of the bookmark.

ACTIVITY   Close your eyes and guess how long a minute is. Check with a clock. See if you can come within 15 seconds, then within 10 seconds, then within 5 seconds. Record how close you come each time.

ACTIVITY   Look at your classroom. Guess its length, its width, and its height. Check your guesses by using a tape measure or other measuring devices.

Drawings can also be used to provide students with practice in estimating skills. Figures 3–11 and 3–12 will give the students an opportunity to estimate. In each case, they should establish a reference base.

This jar contains 10 ounces of oil.

How many ounces of oil does this jar contain?

(Answer: 20 ounces)

Figure 3-11

The tightrope walker has walked 20 feet.
How many more feet must he walk to
reach the other side?
(Answer: 40 feet more)

Figure 3-12

Activities such as these will help your students to improve their ability to estimate answers. Most of all, such practice will encourage them to "take a guesstimate." In itself, this is an important part of problem solving.

11. Encourage your students to use a calculator.

Over 200 million hand-held calculators have been sold in the United States. The majority of your students probably either own a calculator or have access to one owned by someone within their immediate household. A teacher can provide conceptual experience long before the student makes the generalization, and concepts can often be extended to the real world through the use of the calculator. All students can add, subtract, multiply, and divide with a calculator. They can work with problems that are interesting and significant, even though the computations may be beyond their paper-and-pencil capacity. The focus can now be on problem solving for problem solving's sake; strategies and processes can be emphasized, with less time devoted to the computation within the problem-solving context.

PROBLEM   What is the largest whole number you can multiply by 6 and still have a product less than 79?

Discussion   Students can readily multiply each of the numbers in turn, beginning with 1 × 6, 2 × 6, etc., until they find a product that is more than 78.

PROBLEM In the given array find the number that is missing. (*Note:* This is an array of numbers whose rows and columns should all add up to the same sum.)

211	121	181
145	?	205
157	229	127

PROBLEM A gross of pencils is 144 pencils. If each pencil is 18 centimeters long, how long would the line be if all the pencils in a gross were put end to end?

Discussion Students should decide whether their answer will be a number of pencils or a number of centimeters. Once they have decided what to do, the operation may be done easily with a calculator. Suppose the students form a regular 100-gon. What is its perimeter? (*Note:* This can be extended to an area problem.)

PROBLEM Juanita likes to give her answers in large numbers. When asked her age, she replied that she has been alive a total of 7,358,400 minutes. How many years has Juanita been alive? (Consider a year as having 365 days.)

Discussion The students will have to change the minutes to hours, the hours to days, and the days to years. What operation(s) will these calculations involve? Suppose Juanita decided to give her age in seconds. For how many seconds has she been alive?

PROBLEM A major hamburger chain sold 22 billion hamburgers, each 1 inch thick. If we stacked these hamburgers, how many miles high would the stack be?

Discussion Since the number 22 billion has 11 digits, it will not fit on most calculator displays. Hence students might multiply 5,280 by 12 to find out how many hamburgers there are in 1 mile. This number is then divided into 22 billion to get the answer 347,222.22 miles.

12. Take advantage of computer programming.

Schools are rapidly including courses in computer literacy, awareness, and programming in their curriculum. The programming of a computer draws upon many of the skills that are used in problem solving. When students are asked to write a program, they must analyze the task at hand, draw upon their previous knowledge and experiences, and put together an organized plan of steps, operations, and commands that yield the correct results. The format of a program is very much like the heuristics pattern of problem solving.

EXAMPLE   Write a program for finding the area of a rectangle given its length and width.

In order to do this, the student must know what a program is, what a rectangle is, and what is meant by length, width, and area. In other words, he or she must understand what is being asked and what is given. This is exactly the same as the first phases of the problem-solving process.

The student must now review his or her knowledge of area and rectangles to find the proper formula. Now this information is synthesized and the program written.* (This carries the student through the "Solve" phase.)

```
5    HOME

10   REM AREA OF A RECTANGLE

20   PRINT "TYPE IN THE LENGTH IN INCHES."

30   INPUT L

35   PRINT

40   PRINT "TYPE IN THE WIDTH IN INCHES."

50   INPUT W

55   PRINT:PRINT

60   LET A = L * W

70   PRINT "THE AREA OF THE RECTANGLE IS "; A ; "SQUARE INCHES"

80   END
```

*This program is written for the Apple computer.

The student now runs the program. Does it work? (This is "Review.")
If not, why not? If it does run correctly, how could it be modified to
extend it to other geometric figures? (Extend)

13. Have your students flow-chart their own problem-solving process.

Students should realize that they are gradually developing their own set
of heuristics, or problem-solving techniques. They should be made to
recognize the components of their strategy. Therefore, after students
have gone through the problem-solving process several times, ask them
to list and then to flow-chart the steps they have used. At first, the
flowchart might be a simple one, like the one in Figure 3–13.

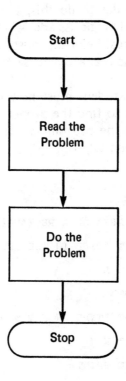

Figure 3–13

However, as the problem-solving process continues to develop, the
flowchart should become more complex, like the one in Figure 3–14.
Notice that the students are now beginning to ask themselves
questions. This is extremely important in the problem-solving process,
as we have stated before.

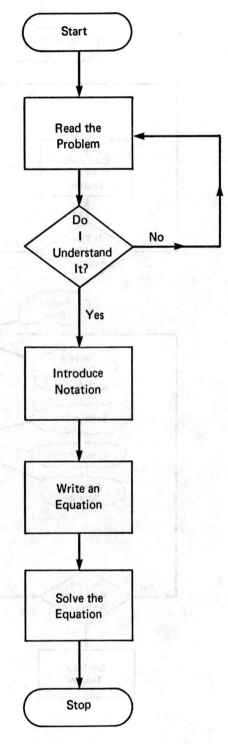

Figure 3–14

After more and more experiences with the problem-solving process, a student might evolve a problem-solving flowchart like the one in Figure 3–15.

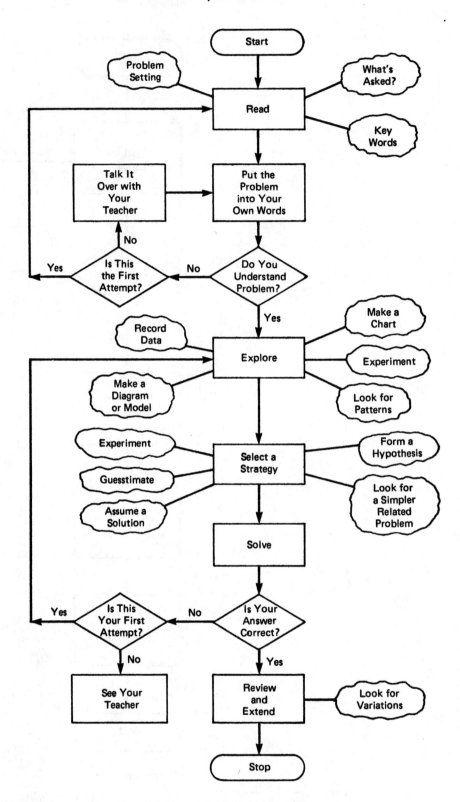

Figure 3-15

The preparation of a flowchart for problem solving is an extremely valuable procedure for both the students and the teacher. It will help the students to better organize their own thoughts. (We feel that anyone who cannot flow-chart a process does not really understand that process.) At the same time, it will provide the teacher with a chance to examine the problem-solving process as the students perceive it. It is a visual example of what the students are thinking as they solve a problem.

14. Use strategy games in class.

Research has shown that students who have been involved in the playing of strategy games have improved their problem-solving ability. This section discusses the use of these strategy games as a vehicle for teaching problem solving. These are *not* games which necessarily involve arithmetic skills, Rather, to be considered a strategy game, the game must meet the following conditions:

1. The game must have a definite set of rules for the players.
2. The game must be played by at least two players, each of whom has a goal; these goals must be in conflict with each other.
3. The players must make "intelligent" choices of moves, based upon whatever information is available at the time of the move.
4. Each player tries to "stop" the opponent from achieving his or her goal before doing so himself.

Notice that "luck" per se or "chance" should play a minimal role in strategy gaming.

Games have a strong appeal for children and adults alike. In fact, most people enjoy games. Witness the many books of puzzles and games that are sold in bookstores, and the puzzle and game sections that appear on napkins in restaurants or in magazines on the airlines. Currently a new wave of strategy games utilizing a microprocessor is appearing.

Children have been exposed to games and gaming all of their lives. They have learned what a game is, that games have rules to be followed, and that it is often possible to win a particular game consistently by developing a strategy to follow. Most of your students are already familiar with some of the basic strategy games, such as tic-tac-toe, checkers, and chess. They already know some basic strategies for these games.

To students, games are real-world problem situations. They want to win! And they enjoy playing games. Remember that skills which are acquired under enjoyable conditions are usually retained for longer periods of time than are skills acquired under stress or other adverse conditions.

When we develop a strategy for winning at a strategy game, we usually go through a series of steps that closely parallel those used in a heuristic system for solving problems.

Strategy Gaming

1. Read the game rules. Understand the play of the game. What is a "move"? What pieces are used? What does the board look like? What is a "win"? When is a game over?
2. Correlate the rules with those from any related game. Is there a similar game whose strategy you know? Select several possible lines of play to follow in an attempt to win the game.
3. Carry out your line of play. Can you counter your opponent's moves as the game proceeds?
4. Look back. If your strategy produced a win, will it work every time? Try alternative lines of play, alternative moves.

The similarity between this sequence and the one we suggested in Chapter 2 is marked indeed.

In order to use strategy games effectively with your students, you need a variety of games. These games can be found in many places. Best of all, games already known to the students can be varied by changing the rules, the pieces, or the game board. In these cases, students need not spend an inordinate amount of time learning all about a "new" game, but can immediately move on to developing a strategy for the play.

PROBLEM   Most of your students already know the game of tic-tac-toe. Under the usual rules, the player who first gets three of his or her own marks (usually X's and O's) in a straight line, either vertically, horizontally, or diagonally, is the winner. A simple rule change might be that the first player who gets three of his or her own marks in a straight line is the loser. This creates an entirely new line of play and requires a different strategy.

When you use these games with your students, have them analyze their play. Have them record their moves in each game. You can help them in this analysis by asking key questions such as:

1. Is it advantageous to go first?
2. Is it advantageous to play a defensive game?
3. If you won, was it luck? Or, will your strategy produce a win again?

Have the students play each game several times. Have them refine their strategy each time. Discuss with the class those strategies that consistently lead to a "win."

You can find many examples of strategy games in a local toy store or by looking through the many game and puzzle books available in bookstores. A brief collection of strategy games has been suggested in Section A.

15. Include problems that have more than one step.

Students have difficulty with problems that involve more than one step in their solution. Thus it is important that students recognize when a problem is embedded within another problem.

EXAMPLE   John bought a hamburger for $1.65 and a soft drink for 89¢. How much did he spend altogether?

This is an example of a one-step problem. The student merely adds $1.65 and .89 to obtain the answer, $2.54. However, we can make this into a two-step problem as follows:

EXAMPLE   John bought a hamburger for $1.65 and a soft drink for 89¢. How much change does he receive from a $5 bill?

Just as before, the student must find out how much John spent altogether. This is sometimes referred to as a "hidden question." It is not asked directly, but the result is needed in order to solve the final problem as it was asked.

ACTIVITY   Present your students with a sheet of problems which are all simple, one-step problems. Ask them to change each into a two-step problem by adding a statement and a new question. At the same time, the original question asked must be removed, although it is kept as a hidden question. Some samples follow.

Single step   Admission to the dog show is $5 for adults. There were 20 adults at the show on Saturday. How much did these adults pay?

Two step   Admission to the dog show is $5 for adults. There were 20 adults at the show on Saturday. On Saturday, they took in $137 in admissions. How much money was collected from people other than adults?

Single step   Ramona has 5 fish tanks. If each tank uses 4 pounds of gravel, how much gravel does Ramona need?

Two step   Ramona has 5 fish tanks. If each tank uses 4 pounds of gravel, and she spent $3.60 for gravel, how much does gravel cost per pound?

ACTIVITY   Give your students several problems with more than one step. In each case, have them identify the hidden question. For example,

Dr. L scored 33 points in last night's basketball game. He scored 13 field goals worth 2 points each, and the rest in foul shots worth 1 point each. How many foul shots did he make?

Hidden question: How many points did he score in field goals?

Jan bought 5 record albums at $7.95 each. The sales tax was 6%. How much was the tax on her albums?

Hidden question: How much was the total cost of the 5 albums before tax?

16. Don't teach new mathematics while teaching problem solving.

The development of the problem-solving process, not the mathematics involved, is the paramount reason for including problem solving in the curriculum. The textbook exercises, labeled "verbal problems," are primarily intended to practice a mathematical skill. Such a focus can easily mask the problem-solving aspect of the activity. Try to keep the mathematics involved in your problems well within the students' level of ability. In some cases, find problems where the math is a relatively minor part of the activity.

PROBLEM   Three boxes each contain a number of billiard balls. One box contains only even-numbered billiard balls, one box contains only odd-numbered billiard balls, and the third box contains a mixture of odd- and even-numbered billiard balls. *All* of the boxes are mislabeled. By selecting one ball from one of the boxes, can you correctly label the three boxes? Why or why not?

Discussion   One approach to the solution of this problem is to identify all the possible cases and try them. The other method is to recognize that, if you draw an even-numbered ball from the box labeled "odd," it might belong either to the box containing only even-numbered balls or to the box containing balls with both odd and even numbers. Because of the symmetry of the cases, selecting an odd-numbered ball from the box labeled "even" would create the same doubt. Thus, by selecting a ball from the box labeled "mixed" we can solve the problem. If the ball has an even number, the box must be relabeled "even," since the "mixed" label must be incorrect. Thus the box labeled "odd" must be relabeled "mixed," and the box labeled "even" must be relabeled "odd." Analogous reasoning is used to discuss the relabeling process if an odd-numbered ball is selected from the box originally labeled "mixed."

PROBLEM   Sixteen teams are entered in a basketball elimination tournament. Winners play winners until only 1 team is left. What is the total number of games that must be played?

Discussion   This problem can be done by setting up an elimination diagram, as in Figure 3–16.

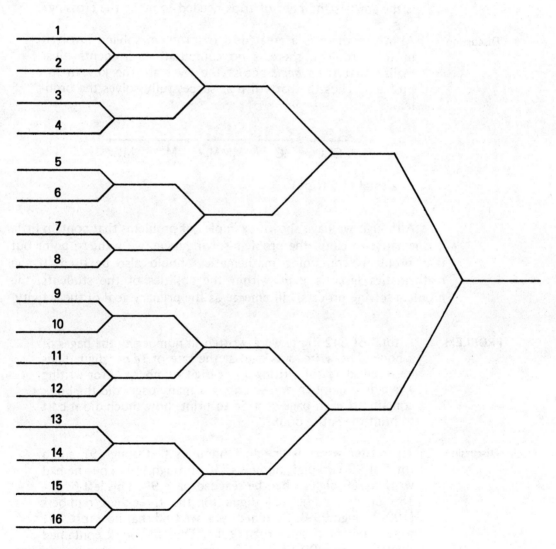

Number of games: 8   +   4   +   2   +   1   =   15

Figure 3–16

There is another more artistic solution to this problem, however. Since 1 team is eliminated in each game played and we must eliminate 15 teams, 15 games are needed to leave 1 team the final winner.

PROBLEM Three missionaries and three cannibals wish to cross a river. There is a boat that can carry up to three people, and either the missionaries or the cannibals can operate the boat. However, it is never permissible for the cannibals to outnumber the missionaries, either in the boat or on either shore. What is the smallest number of trips needed to make the crossing?

Discussion Although there is a great deal of problem solving involved in this problem, there is no computation. Students must realize that trips *back* across the river are the key to the problem. Thus the pattern that successfully solves the problem is

$$\xrightarrow{\hspace{2cm}} \xleftarrow{\hspace{2cm}} \xrightarrow{\hspace{2cm}} \xleftarrow{\hspace{2cm}} \xrightarrow{\hspace{2cm}}$$

CCC   C   MMM   M   MC

or a total of 5 trips.

Although we have shown examples of problems that contain little mathematics to cloud the problem-solving issue, we want to point out that problems containing mathematics should also be used. If the mathematics level is kept within the abilities of the students, the problem-solving process will emerge as the primary goal of the activity.

PROBLEM A total of 642 digits were written in numbering the pages of a book. The writer was paid at the rate of 1¢ per digit. Thus he received 1¢ for writing a one-digit number, 2¢ for writing a two-digit number, and so on. How many pages did the book contain? If each page cost 5¢ to print, how much did it cost to print the entire book?

Discussion The writer wrote 9 one-digit numbers (1 through 9), and a total of 90 two-digit numbers (10 through 99). Thus he had written 189 digits when he reached page 99. This left 642 — 189 or 453 additional digits for the three-digit numbers (100 through 999). Dividing by 3, we find that he wrote 151 page numbers of three digits each. Thus the book contained a total of 151 + 90 + 9 or 250 pages.

Notice that the mathematics in this problem probably would not be too difficult for the average eighth or ninth grader to follow. Thus the problem-solving process could easily be emphasized, without being "cluttered up" by the mathematics.

SECTION A

A Collection of
Strategy Games

TIC-TAC-TOE VARIATIONS

Since the basic game of tic-tac-toe is already known to most students, it becomes a logical place to find a wide assortment of variations.

1. Reverse Tic-Tac-Toe

This game has already been described in Chapter 3. It simply changes the requirements for a "win." Students must take turns placing an X or an O on the board, and try to *avoid* getting three marks in a row.

2. Triangular Tic-Tac-Toe

This game uses the basic rule—that is, the player scoring three of his or her marks in a straight line is the winner. The playing surface, however, has been changed into the triangular array shown in Figure A–1, rather than the usual square array.

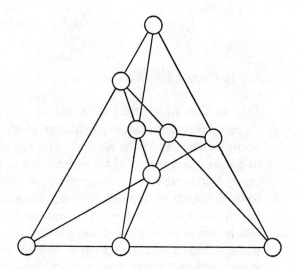

Figure A–1. The Playing Board for Triangular Tic-Tac-Toe

3. Put 'Em Down Tic-Tac-Toe

Instead of making marks on a tic-tac-toe board, each player is provided with three markers or other playing pieces. These are alternately placed on any of the line intersections (circles) on the playing surface in Figure A–2. The center circle may *not* be used by either player as his or her first play. After all the playing pieces have been placed, each player in turn moves one of his or her own pieces along a line to the next vacant cell. The winner is the first player to get three of his or her own pieces in a row, either vertically, horizontally, or diagonally.

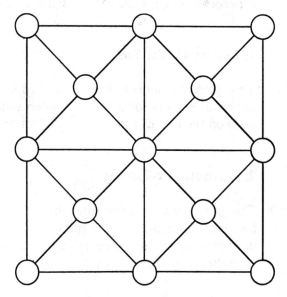

Figure A–2. The Playing Board for Put 'Em Down Tic-Tac-Toe

4. Point Score Tic-Tac-Toe

This version of tic-tac-toe is played on a 25-square playing surface. Players take turns placing a marker of an identifiable color in any un-occupied square on the surface. The object of the game is for a player to get as many pieces of his or her own color as possible in a row (verti-cally, horizontally, or diagonally). A playing piece is counted in all rows in which it appears. Players score 1 point for three in a row, 2 points for four in a row, 5 points for five in a row. When the square board is completely filled up, players total up their scores to find the winner. The diagram in Figure A–3 shows the playing surface for the game, with a 1-point and 2-point score (horizontally and diagonally, respectively). Notice how one marker counts twice, once in each row.

5. Wild Card Tic-Tac-Toe

This version of tic-tac-toe is played on the traditional 3 x 3 square array commonly used in tic-tac-toe. The variation in this version allows either player to put either mark anywhere on the playing surface when his or her turn comes. (Either an X or an O may be placed by either player at any time during the game.) The winner is the player who *completes* a straight line of three marks of either kind in his or her turn.

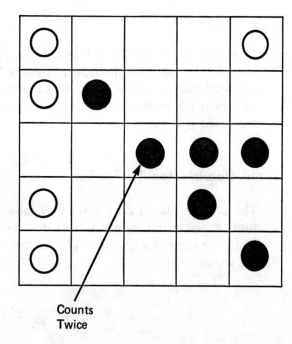

Counts
Twice

Figure A–3. The Playing Board for Point Score Tic-Tac-Toe

6. Three-Person Tic-Tac-Toe

Most versions of tic-tac-toe are games between two players. In this version, however, three people play. Players use either an X, an O, or an I as a marker, and the game is played on a board that contains 6 x 6 or 36 squares. Players put their own mark anywhere on the playing surface in turn. The first player to get three of his or her own marks in a row is the winner.

7. Big 7 Tic-Tac-Toe

This game is played on a playing surface consisting of 49 squares in a 7 x 7 array. Two players take turns placing either an X or an O anywhere on the playing surface. Each places his or her own mark. The first player to get four marks in a row is the winner.

8. Double Trouble Tic-Tac-Toe

This game is played on a 25-square (5 x 5) board. Players take turns placing either two X's or two O's anywhere on the board. The first player to get four of his or her marks in a row horizontally, vertically, or diagonally is the winner.

9. As You Wish Tic-Tac-Toe

This game is played on a 25-square (5 x 5) playing surface. Each player in turn may place on the board as many X's or O's as he or she wishes, provided they are all in the same vertical or horizontal row. The player who puts his or her mark into the twenty-fifth or last vacant cell on the board is the winner.

10. Dots-in-a-Row Tic-Tac-Toe

The game is played on a surface as shown in Figure A-4. Players take turns crossing out as many dots as they desire, provided the dots all lie in the same straight line. The player who crosses out the last dot is the winner.

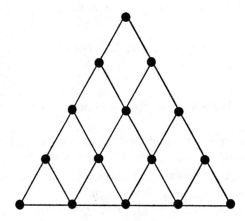

Figure A-4. The Dots-in-a-Row Board

11. Tac-Tic-Toe

This game is played on a 4 x 4 square surface. Each player has four chips or markers of a single color. The starting position is shown in Figure A-5. Players take turns moving a single piece of their own color. A move consists of moving one piece onto a vacant square either horizontally or vertically, but not diagonally. There is no jumping or capturing in this game. No piece can be moved into an already occupied square, but must be moved into an open, adjacent square. The player who moves three of his or her own pieces into a row, either horizontally, vertically, or diagonally, with no intervening spaces or intervening squares occupied by an opponent's piece, is the winner.

80

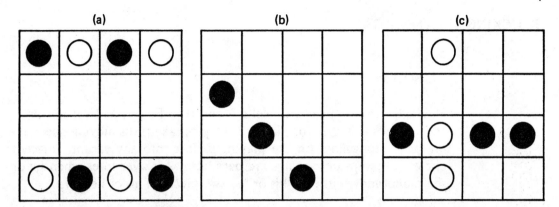

Figure A–5. (a) Starting Position for Tic-Tac-Toe. (b) A Win Position for Tic-Tac-Toe. (c) Nobody Wins in These Positions.

12. Tac-Tic-Toe, Chinese Version

This game is played on the surface shown in Figure A–6. Players use four chips, each player having a different color. Starting position is as shown in Figure A–6. Each player may move only his or her own chips. A move involves placing one of one's own pieces into an adjacent, vacant cell, following the lines on the board. There is no jumping and no capturing. The player who places three of his or her own pieces in the same straight line, with no vacant spaces intervening and none of the opponent's pieces intervening, is the winner.

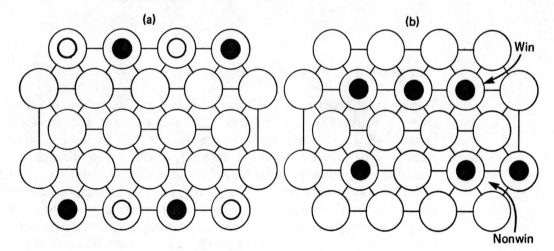

Figure A–6. (a) Starting Position for Tac-Tic-Toe, Chinese Version. (b) A Winning Position and a Nonwinning Position.

BLOCKING STRATEGY GAMES

13. Blockade

Playing pieces are placed on cells A and B in Figure A-7 for player 1, and on cells C and D for player 2. Players take turns moving one playing piece along lines on the playing surface into any vacant, adjacent circle. No jumps or captures are permitted. A player loses when he or she cannot move either of his or her two pieces in his or her turn.

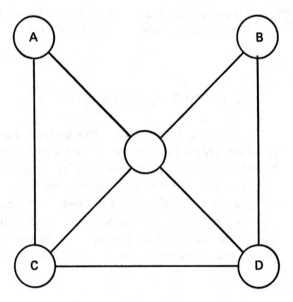

Figure A-7. Playing Surface for Blockade

14. Pawns

This game is played on a 3 x 3 array of squares. Each player has three chips or markers of a single color. Starting position is as shown in Figure A-8. Players take turns moving one of their own pieces. Each piece may be moved one square forward, or one square diagonally if a capture is made. A diagonal move can be made *only* with a capture, and a capture cannot be made on a forward move. A captured piece is removed from the board. A player is a winner when he or she either (1) places one piece in the opponent's starting row, or (2) makes the last possible move on the playing board. As a variation, players can play the game on a 4 x 4 or a 5 x 5 board, with an adjusted number of pieces.

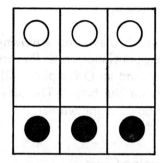

Figure A-8. Starting Position for Pawns

15. Hex

The game of Hex is played on a diamond-shaped board made up of hexagons. (See Figure A-9.) The players take turns placing an X or an O in any hexagon on the board. The winner is the first player to make an unbroken path from one side of the board to the other. Blocking moves and other strategies should be developed as the game proceeds. The corner hexagons can belong to either player.

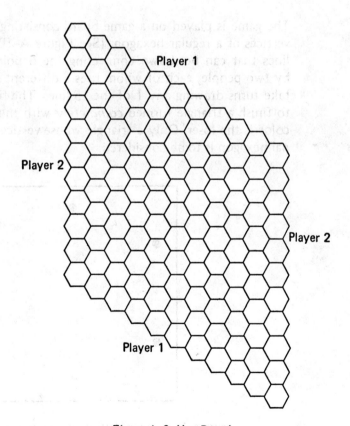

Figure A-9. Hex Board

16. Bi-Squares

The game is played on a playing surface that consists of 16 squares in one long continuous row. Players take turns placing their mark (an X for player 1 and an O for player 2) into each of two adjacent, unoccupied squares on the board. The player who makes the last successful move on the board is the winner.

17. Domino Cover

This game is played on a standard 8 x 8 checkerboard, and uses a set of dominoes that will cover two adjacent squares, either horizontally or vertically. Players take turns placing a domino anywhere on the board, according to the following rules: (1) player 1 can only place dominoes in a horizontal direction; (2) player 2 can only place dominoes in a vertical direction. The loser is the player who cannot make a move by placing a domino in the correct position.

18. Triahex

The game is played on a game board consisting of 6 points that are the vertices of a regular hexagon. (See Figure A–10.) There are exactly 15 lines that can be drawn connecting the 6 points. The game is played by two people, each of whom uses a different colored marker. Players take turns drawing any 1 of the 15 lines. The first player who is forced to finish a triangle formed *completely* with the lines of his or her own color is the loser. Only a triangle whose vertices are points of the original hexagon is to be considered.

Figure A–10. The Six Vertices of a Regular Hexagon in Triahex

19. Dodge 'Em

The game is played on a 3 x 3 square board with two black checkers and two white ones. Starting position is shown in Figure A-11. Black sits on the south side of the board, white on the west side. Players may move a checker forward or to their left or right, unless the checker is blocked by another counter of either color or the edge of the playing surface. Each player's goal is to move all of his or her pieces off the far side of the board. Black moves north, west, or east, and tries to move all of his or her pieces off the board on the north side; white moves east, north, or south, and tries to move his or her pieces off the board on the east side. There are no captures or jumps. A player must always leave the opponent a legal move or forfeit the game. The first player to get his or her two pieces off the board is the winner.

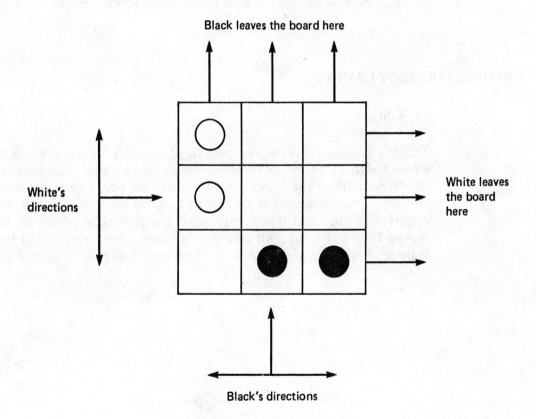

Figure A-11. A Dodge 'Em Board

20. Tromino Saturation

The game is played on a 5 x 5 square board. The playing pieces consist of the two basic tromino shapes shown in Figure A-12. Each tromino piece should exactly cover three squares on the playing surface. Players take turns placing one of the pieces of either shape anywhere on the playing surface. The first player who cannot place a piece to exactly cover three squares is the loser. (In order to allow each player a full choice of which piece to select on each play, prepare eight pieces of each kind.) If the size of the board is increased to a 6 x 6 square board, prepare twelve of each piece.

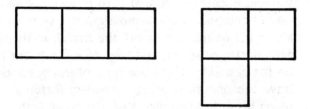

Figure A-12. The Two Basic Tromino Shapes for Saturation

CAPTURE STRATEGY GAMES

21. Solitaire

This is a strategy game for one person. The playing surface consists of a board with 15 circles, as shown in Figure A-13. Place chips or other counters on all of the cells except the darkened cell. The player must remove as many counters as possible by jumping counters over adjacent counters (along lines) into empty cells. The jumped counters are removed from the board. All counters but one can be removed in this manner. A winning game is one in which only one counter remains. A

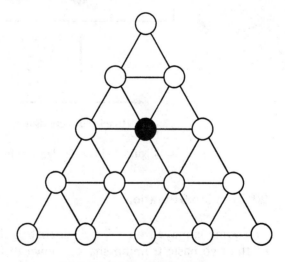

Figure A-13. A Solitaire Board

variation for experienced players is to try to make the one remaining counter end the game in the darkened cell.

22. Spot

Spot is played on a circular playing surface, as shown in Figure A-14. Place a penny on spot 2, a dime on spot 15. Players take turns; one moves the penny, the other moves the dime. Moves are made along any solid line into an adjacent spot. The penny moves first. The object of the game is for the penny to "capture" the dime by moving into the spot the dime occupies. The capture must be made within six moves. The penny player loses if he or she has failed to catch the dime by the end of his or her sixth move.

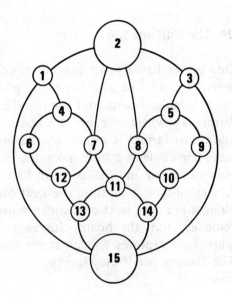

Figure A-14. A Spot Playing Surface

23. Fox and Geese

This game, for two players, is played on a surface with 33 cells, as shown in Figure A-15. The fox marker and the thirteen goose markers are placed as shown. The fox can move in any direction along a line— up, down, left, or right. The geese may not move backwards. The fox can capture a goose by making a short jump over a single goose along a line into the next cell, provided that cell is vacant. The fox can make successive jumps on any one turn, provided vacant cells exist. The geese win if they can corner the fox so that he cannot move. The fox wins if he captures enough geese so that they cannot corner him.

87

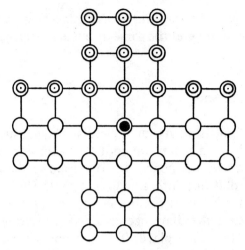

Figure A-15. Starting Position for Fox and Geese

24. The Wolf and the Farmers

One player has a single playing piece, the wolf. The other player has seven farmers. The wolf begins by placing his piece on the top circle of the triangular board in Figure A-16. The second player places one farmer anywhere else on the board. Each time the wolf moves, an additional farmer is placed on the board. All pieces move the same way, one circle at a time, along the marked lines. However, the farmers may not move until all of them have been entered on the board. The farmers may not capture; the wolf captures by jumping over a farmer along a line to a next cell, which must be vacant. The jumped piece is removed from the board. Successive captures are allowed. The wolf wins if he captures enough farmers so that they cannot confine him. The farmers win if they succeed in confining the wolf so that he cannot move.

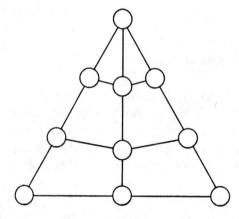

Figure A-16. Playing Surface for the Wolf and the Farmers

25. Sprouts

Three dots are placed in a triangular array on a piece of paper. Players take turns drawing a line connecting any two dots, or connecting a dot to itself. After a line is drawn, a new dot is placed approximately midway between the two dots being connected, along the connecting line. No lines may cross, and no more than three lines may terminate in a single point. The last player to make a successful move is the winner. See Figure A-17. The new point D is shown along the line connecting point A to itself. The new point E is shown along the line connecting B to C. Notice that points D, A, and E each have two lines terminating.

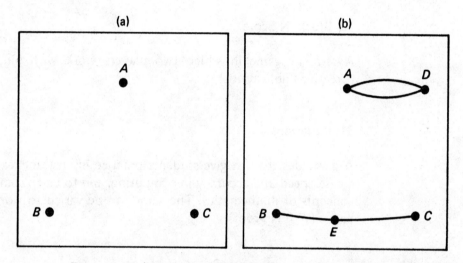

Figure A-17. (a) A Sprouts Board. (b) Typical Moves in Sprouts

26. Square-Off

The game is played on a checkerboard. Two players take turns placing one checker anywhere on the board. Each player uses checkers of one color. The game continues until the checkers of one color form the vertices of a square of any size. The player using that color is declared the winner.

SOME COMMERCIAL STRATEGY GAMES

27. Basis

A strategy game in which players form numerals in different bases, while preventing their opponents from doing the same. (Holt, Rinehart and Winston Company)

28. Battleship

A game of strategy in which two players try to sink each other's ships, which are hidden from view. A good introduction to coordinates. (Creative Publications)

29. Bee Line

Players use strategy while attempting to make a "beeline" across the playing board. (SEE Corporation)

30. Block 'N Score

A strategy game in which two players work with binary notation. (Creative Publications)

31. Equations

A game designed to give students practice in abstract reasoning, to increase speed and accuracy in computing, and to teach some of the basic concepts of mathematics. The game can be varied to work in different bases. (Wff 'N Proof)

32. Foo (Fundamental Order of Operations)

A strategy game in which players try to combine seven cards into any multiple of 12. Extra cards are drawn and discarded until one player calls "Foo!" (Cuisenaire, Inc.)

33. Helix

Another three-dimensional tic-tac-toe game. Players place different colored beads on a series of pins, trying to get four in a row. The pins are not only in straight lines, but also along arcs designated on the playing surface. (Creative Publications)

34. Kalah

A strategy game involving counting, skill, and logic. Chance is a minimal factor. (Creative Publications)

35. Mastermind

A secret code of colored pegs is set up out of sight of one player. He or she then has ten chances to duplicate the colors and exact positions of the code pegs. Pure logic! (Cadaco, Invicta, Creative Publications)

36. Numble

A game similar to a crossword puzzle. Players place tiles with numerals from 0 to 9 on them to form addition, subtraction, multiplication, and division problems. (Math Media, Inc.)

37. On Sets

A series of games that teach some of the basic ideas of set theory and set language. Comes with an excellent manual. Involves union, intersection, complement, etc. (Wff 'N Proof)

38. Pressups

A player must guide the direction of play so as to press down pegs of his or her own color. Traps may be set. The winner is the player with more of his or her own pegs depressed. (Invicta)

39. Qubic

Qubic expands tic-tac-toe into a four-level space game. Players win by setting four markers in a straight line in one or several planes. (Parker Brothers)

40. Racko

By drawing from the pile players attempt to replace cards in their racks so that the numbers read from high to low in numerical sequence. (Milton Bradley Company)

41. Score Four

Similar to Qubic and Helix. Players place wooden beads on metal pins and need four in a row to score. (Lakeside Toys)

42. Soma Cube

An elegant cube with irregular sets of combinations of cubes. There are 1,105,920 mathematically different ways to come up with the 240 ways the seven SOMA pieces fit together to form the original cube. (Parker Brothers)

43. Tromino

Triangular wooden pieces extend the skills and principles needed for dominoes. A great deal of strategy is used as well as mathematical knowledge. (Creative Publications)

44. Tuf

A game designed to help students utilize the basic operations of mathematics. Students form equations using tiles with various numerals and operations on them. Both speed and accuracy count. (Avalon Hill Company)

45. Twixt

A board strategy game with moves and countermoves. Players try to connect a chain of linked pegs before their opponents can do the same. (3-M Company)

46. Vectors

A game in which thought and ability are used to deceive opponents. The game utilizes a chess-like board with a single piece and cards. (Cuisenaire, Inc.)

47. Wff 'N Proof

The game is based on symbolic logic. Symbols are used to form logical sequences. (Wff 'N Proof)

SECTION B

A Collection of
Non-Routine Problems

Problems 1–30 are particularly applicable to the elementary school student. Problems 31–70 are particularly applicable to the junior high school student. Problems 71–110 are particularly applicable to the senior high school student. Problems marked with an asterisk are easily adaptable to other levels.

PROBLEM 1   July 4 is a Tuesday. Your birthday is on July 23rd. On what day of the week is your birthday?

Discussion   A good way of attacking this problem is to sketch a calendar for the month. The answer is easily found this way. An alternative method without drawing the calendar is to use the fact that a week contains 7 days. Thus July 11, 18 and 25 are all Tuesdays. Counting back from July 25 to July 23 places the birthday on a Sunday.

PROBLEM 2   Lonny has 2 bats and 1 ball that cost her $11. Andy has 1 bat and 2 balls that cost him $7. How much does 1 bat and 1 ball cost?

Discussion   Guess and test! The cost of 1 bat is $5 and the cost of 1 ball is $1.

PROBLEM 3   What is the sum of the numbers in this table?

3/4	3/8	3/7	3/5	3/13
2/5	4/7	10/13	5/8	1/4

Discussion   A careful examination of the table reveals that there are five pairs of fractions whose sum is 1. Thus the sum of the ten numbers is 5.

PROBLEM 4   How many different ways can you make change for a 50¢ piece without using pennies?

Discussion   In order to organize the work, prepare a table.

Nickels (5¢)	Dimes (10¢)	Quarters (25¢)
10	0	0
9	–	– (cannot be done)
8	1	0
7	–	– (cannot be done)
6	2	0
5	0	1
4	3	0
3	1	1
2	4	0
1	2	1
0	5	0
0	0	2

Thus there are a total of 10 ways to satisfy the given conditions.

PROBLEM 5   You are waiting for the elevator to take you to a restaurant on the 70th floor of the Hancock building. There are 45 people in line ahead of you. If each elevator can carry 10 people, on which trip will you be?

Discussion   The fact that the restaurant is on the 70th floor is excess information. If 10 people go on each trip, the first four trips of the elevator will take 40 people. You will be on the 5th trip. Some children may begin with 46 and repeatedly subtract 10.

PROBLEM 6   Peter, Paul, and Mary have 5 cookies. How many ways can they divide the cookies if each person must get at least one cookie?

Discussion   Make a table:

Peter	Paul	Mary
1	3	1
1	2	2
1	1	3
2	1	2
2	2	1
3	1	1

There are 6 ways it can be done.

96

A Collection of Non-Routine Problems

PROBLEM 7 The new game in town is an addition game known as Eighteen. Players take turns placing a chip or marker on one of the numbers from 2 through 10. The first player to cover any three numbers whose sum is 18 is the winner. Jeff understands the game and has figured out a method so that he can never lose. (He may have a game end in a tie, however.) How does Jeff do this?

Discussion Although the numbers in the Eighteen game are arranged in a row, Jeff, in his head, has placed the numbers in a typical magic square arrangement, as shown.

7	2	9
8	6	4
3	10	5

As the game is played, Jeff views it as a tic-tac-toe board. He plays either to win or to block. If he can play tic-tac-toe to win, then he can easily win at Eighteen.

PROBLEM 8 Nancy had 69¢ in coins. Jill asked her for change for a half-dollar. Nancy tried to make change, but found that she didn't have the correct coins to do so. What coins did she have, if each coin was less than a half-dollar?

Discussion Trial and error will enable students to find that the coins were 1 quarter, 4 dimes, and 4 pennies.

PROBLEM 9 A football team won 3 more games than it lost. The team played 11 games. How many games did they lose?

Discussion Some students may solve this problem using the guess-and-test strategy. Others may subtract the 3 games, to make the number of wins and losses equal. Then divide (11 − 3) by 2 to get 4 losses.

PROBLEM 10 Given the sequence of numbers

2, 3, 5, 8

explain why the next number might be 12, or 13, or 2.

Discussion There are a variety of ways in which the four given terms might have been arrived at. For example, if we regard these as members of a Fibonacci sequence, each term was arrived at by adding the preceding two terms. Thus, $2 + 3 = 5$, $3 + 5 = 8$, $5 + 8 = 13$, and so on. On the other hand, we might view the sequence as having been generated by adding increasing differences. Thus $2 + 1 = 3$, $3 + 2 = 5$, $5 + 3 = 8$, $8 + 4 = 12$, and so on. Then, too, this might be viewed as a cyclical series in which the four terms repeat. Thus the next term would be 2.

PROBLEM 11   What is the greatest number of coins you can use to make 35¢? What is the smallest number of coins you can use? In how many different ways can you make 35¢?

Discussion   The greatest number of coins is obviously 35 pennies. The smallest number of coins is 2 (1 dime, 1 quarter). To find the number of different ways change can be made, we can make a table.

Pennies	Nickels	Dimes	Quarters
35	—	—	—
30	1	—	—
25	—	1	—
25	2	—	—
.	.	.	.
.	.	.	.
.	.	.	.
—	—	1	1

PROBLEM 12   A woman has some cows and some chickens. Together the animals have a total of 54 legs. How many cows and how many chickens might she have?

Discussion   We have the restriction that cows have 4 legs and chickens have only 2 legs. Since 54 is not evenly divisible by 4, she must have at least 1 chicken. We now form a table to organize our results:

Cows	Legs	Chickens	Legs	Total number of legs
13	52	1	2	54
12	48	2	4	54
11	44	5	10	54
etc.				

We might extend the question by asking if it is possible to have exactly 3 chickens, 4 chickens, etc., and why.

PROBLEM 13

What was the final score of the Tigers-Sharks baseball game?

(a) The sum of their scores was 8.
(b) The product of their scores was 15.
(c) The Sharks won the game.

Discussion

Make a list of all number-pairs whose sum is 8.

$$8 - 0$$
$$7 - 1$$
$$6 - 2$$
$$5 - 3$$
$$4 - 4$$

Now find the pair of numbers whose product is 15. Since the Sharks won the game, the final score must have been Sharks 5, Tigers 3.

PROBLEM 14

A taxi charges 90¢ for the first one-quarter mile and 25¢ for each additional quarter-mile. How much did Leon pay to ride 1 3/4 miles?

Discussion

This is a multi-stage problem. The first quarter mile costs 90¢. This leaves six quarters (Stage 2). These 6 quarters each cost 25¢, or $1.50 (Stage 3). The total cost is $1.50 + .90 or $2.40 (Stage 4).

PROBLEM 15

Two students in the local elementary school have a business selling apples. Each has 30 apples to sell. Allen wants to sell his apples at 5¢ each, while Suzy wants to sell her apples at 3 for 10¢. They decide to merge their operations and to sell all 60 apples at 5 for 20¢. Which way would they make more money, and how much more would they make?

Discussion

Allen would sell his 30 apples at 5¢ each, receiving a total of 30 X .05 or $1.50. Suzy would sell her 30 apples at 3 for 10¢, receiving a total of $1.00. Together they would receive a total of $2.50. If they sell all 60 apples at 5 for 20¢, they will receive a total of $2.40. Thus they would make a profit of 10¢ more by selling the apples in the original manner.

PROBLEM 16

A typical jet plane uses a gallon of gasoline for every 5 miles it flies. If the Dogpatch Airliner travels at 375 miles an hour and has flown for 700 hours, how much gasoline has the airliner used? At 64¢ per gallon, how much has this gasoline cost the airline?

Discussion If we multiply the miles per hour (375) by the number of hours flown (700), we obtain 262,500 miles flown. Dividing this by the number of miles per gallon (5), we obtain a total of 52,500 gallons of gasoline. Now we multiply this by 64¢ to find the total cost: $33,600. (Notice that this is an excellent problem to do with a calculator.)

PROBLEM 17 From Figure B-1 select 2 strips of paper whose lengths have a sum of 15 centimeters and a difference of 3 centimeters.

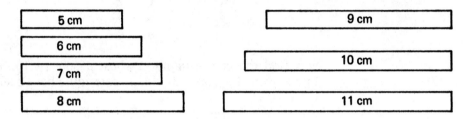

Figure B-1

Discussion Students may begin by examining pairs of paper strips, the sum of whose lengths is 15 centimeters (10, 5; 9, 6; 8, 7), and then check for a difference of 3 centimeters. Others may decide to list all pairs of numbers together with their sums and differences.

PROBLEM 18 What is the smallest number of pennies that can be arranged into 6 equal piles and also into 8 equal piles?

Discussion Some students will multiply 6 × 8 and give 48 as their answer. This would be a correct solution if it were not for the requirement that the answer be the *smallest* number. Thus 24 is the correct answer. Notice that this problem can be done using chips, marbles, or bottlecaps.

PROBLEM 19 Put single digit in each box and make the problem correct.

Discussion   There are two possible answers:

$$
\begin{array}{r}
545 \\
\times\ 2 \\
\hline
1090
\end{array}
\qquad
\begin{array}{r}
218 \\
\times\ 5 \\
\hline
1090
\end{array}
$$

PROBLEM 20   Stanley makes extra money by buying and selling comic books. He buys them for 7¢ each and sells them for 10¢ each. Stanley needs 54¢ to buy some batteries for his calculator. How many comic books must Stanley buy and sell to earn the 54¢?

Discussion   Some students will realize that Stanley earns 3¢ profit on each comic book. Thus they can divide 54¢ by 3¢ to find the number of comic books he must sell (18). Others will want to make a table:

Number of comics	1	2	3	4	5	6	7	...
Profit	3¢	6¢	9¢	12¢	15¢	18¢	21¢	...

PROBLEM 21   Luisa was playing darts. She threw 6 darts, and all 6 hit the target in Figure B-2. Which of the following could be her score?

4, 17, 56, 28, 29, 31

Figure B-2

Discussion   Since all 6 darts hit the target, Luisa's highest score could be 6 X 9 or 54; her lowest score could be 6 X 1 or 6. Furthermore, since there are only odd numbers on the target, the 6 hits must have an even sum. Thus only 28 is a possible score for Luisa. This score can be reached in a variety of ways:

$$9 + 9 + 5 + 3 + 1 + 1 = 28$$
$$9 + 7 + 7 + 3 + 1 + 1 = 28$$

etc.

PROBLEM 22   What's my number?

        (a) I am a two-digit number.
        (b) I am a multiple of 6.
        (c) The sum of my digits is 9.
        (d) My ten's digit is one-half of my unit's digit.

Discussion   Make a progressive list of all numbers that satisfy the first two clues and check each number against the remaining clues.

PROBLEM 23   In a six-day bike race, one team of five riders covered 276 miles. What was the average mileage per day?

Discussion   The number of riders is excess information. Students must divide 276 miles by 6.

PROBLEM 24   Here is a menu for lunch in school:

        Hamburger . . . . .38¢
        French Fries . . . . .15¢
        Malted. . . . . .35¢
        Milk. . . . . .25¢

James spent 78¢. What did he buy?

Discussion   By guess and test, we arrive at 1 hamburger, 1 french fry, and 1 milk. (Ask the students if other answers are possible.)

PROBLEM 25   How many lengths of rope each 3 feet long can be cut from a roll of rope that contains 50 feet?

Discussion   If we divide 50 by 3, we obtain 16 with a remainder of 2. Thus the correct answer is 16. We disregard the remainder.

PROBLEM 26   Draw two straight lines across the face of the clock so that the sum of the numbers in all three regions will be the same.

| Discussion | Since the sum of all the numbers from 1 to 12 is 78, we must draw the lines so that we enclose a total of 78/3 or 26 in each region. Thus |

$$\text{Region } \#1 = 11 + 12 + 1 + 2 = 28$$
$$\text{Region } \#2 = \ 9 + 10 + 3 + 4 = 28$$
$$\text{Region } \#3 = \ 5 + \ 6 + 7 + 8 = 28$$

| PROBLEM 27 | A second-hand comic book store will trade 4 of their books for 5 of yours. How many comic books will you receive for 35 of yours? |

| Discussion | Your 35 books can be divided into 7 groups of 5. You will receive 7 groups of 4 in return. |

| *PROBLEM 28 | If a pound of plums contains 4 to 6 plums, what is the least possible weight in pounds of 3 dozen plums? |

| Discussion | Since a pound will contain 4, 5, or 6 plums, three dozen plums (36 plums) will weigh 9 pounds, 7 1/5 pounds, or 6 pounds. The least possible weight is 6 pounds. |

| *PROBLEM 29 | Mary has scored 98, 65, 63, and 80 on 4 tests this term. What must she score on the next test, if her average is to be 80 for all 5 tests? |

| Discussion | To have an average of 80 on 5 tests, Mary's total must be 5 X 80 or 400. She already has 306 (98 + 65 + 63 + 80). She needs a 94. |

| *PROBLEM 30 | In a class election, the winning candidate received three times as many votes as her opponent. If 32 votes were cast, how many votes did the winner receive? |

| Discussion | Students may do this problem by guess and test. Others may wish to use a simple number sentence: |

$$\square + 3\square = 32$$

| PROBLEM 31 | One day a man entered a shop; he paid 1¢ to get in, spent one-half of the money he had, and then paid 1¢ to leave. He then paid 1¢ to enter a second shop, where he spent one-half of the money he had left and again paid 1¢ to leave. He then entered a third shop, where he again paid 1¢ to get in, spent one-half of the money he had left, and paid 1¢ to |

leave. Finally he entered a fourth shop, where he paid 1¢ to get in, spent one-half of the money he had left, and paid 1¢ to leave. On leaving the fourth shop, he found himself completely broke. How much money had he begun with?

Discussion   The problem lends itself to working backwards:

Shop 4	1¢	to leave
	2¢	spent one-half
	3¢	to enter
Shop 3	4¢	to leave
	8¢	spent one-half
	9¢	to enter
Shop 2	10¢	to leave
	20¢	spent one-half
	21¢	to enter
Shop 1	22¢	to leave
	44¢	spent one-half
	45¢	to enter

He began with 45¢.

*PROBLEM 32   Given the digits 1, 1, 2, 2, 3, 3, 4, 4, write an eight-digit number using these eight digits such that the

1's are separated by 1 digit;

2's are separated by 2 digits;

3's are separated by 3 digits;

4's are separated by 4 digits.

Discussion   Organized guess-and-test should yield several solutions similar to 2 3 4 2 1 3 1 4.

PROBLEM 33   A merchant who was liquidating his stock offered various items at the following prices:

7 items at $10 per item
12 items at $ 8 per item
15 items at $ 6 per item
6 items at $ 5 per item.

If he sold one-half of this stock on the first day, what is the most money he could have received?

Discussion   Since there are a total of 40 items and he sold half, he must have sold 20 items. Selecting the 20 items beginning with the most expensive, we get:

$$7 \text{ items at } \$10 \text{ each} = \$ \ 70$$
$$12 \text{ items at } \$ \ 8 \text{ each} = \$ \ 96$$
$$1 \text{ item at } \$ \ 6 \quad \ \ = \underline{\$ \ \ 6}$$
$$\$172$$

PROBLEM 34   A penny weighs approximately 3 grams. A nickel weighs approximately 5 grams. About how much more does $5 in pennies weigh than $5 in nickels?

Discussion $5 in pennies will be 500 pennies that weigh 1500 grams. $5 in nickels will be 100 nickels that weigh 500 grams. The difference = 1000 grams.

PROBLEM 35   A grocer has three pails: an empty pail that holds 5 liters, an empty pail that holds 3 liters, and an 8-liter pail that is filled with apple cider. Show how the grocer can measure exactly 4 liters of apple cider with the help of the 5-liter and 3-liter pails.

Discussion   Make a chart to show how the grocer might do the division.

3-liter pail	5-liter pail	8-liter pail
0	0	8
0	5	3
3	2	3
3	0	5
0	3	5
3	3	2
1	5	2
1	0	7
0	1	7
3	1	4

While this does yield an answer to the problem, notice that this answer is not a minimum number of pourings (not called for in the original problem). For example, the first three steps can be ignored; one could begin directly with step 4 (3 liters in the 3-liter pail, 5 liters left in the 8-liter pail). Students should be encouraged to go on to find the minimum number of pourings needed.

PROBLEM 36 A customer ordered 15 cupcakes. Cupcakes are placed in packages of 4, 3, or 1. In how many different ways can you fill the order?

Discussion Students can arrange 15 chips or bottlecaps in groups of 4, 3, and 1 to total 15. This can be done in 15 ways:

4's	3's	1's
3	1	0
3	0	3
2	2	1
2	1	4
2	0	7
1	3	2
1	2	5
1	1	8
1	0	11
0	5	0
0	4	3
0	3	6
0	2	9
0	1	12
0	0	15

PROBLEM 37 An old man on his way to market was knocked down. All the eggs he was going to sell were broken. When asked how many eggs he had had, the man replied, "I don't remember the exact number, but when they were put into piles of 2, there was 1 left over; in piles of 3, there was 1 left over. The same was true if I put them into piles of 4, piles of 5, and piles of 6. There was always 1 left over. However, if I put them into piles of 7, there were none left over." How many eggs did the old man have when he started?

Discussion We multiply $2 \times 3 \times 4 \times 5 \times 6$ and obtain 720. Adding the 1 left over, we obtain 721, which is exactly divisible by 7. Thus one possible answer is 721 eggs. However, is this the smallest number? Students might wish to examine all of the multiples of 7 until they can find one that leaves a remainder of 1 when divided by 2, by 3, by 4, by 5, and by 6. The first number that works is 301. Other answers might be revealed in a similar manner.

PROBLEM 38   Which of the following represents the cube of 156?

(a) 3,796,416   (c) 3,944,312
(b) 4,251,528   (d) 3,581,577

Discussion   Many students will simply cube 156 to find the answer. However, they should be encouraged to investigate the pattern that evolves when we cube numbers that have a final digit of 1, 2, 3, 4, etc. Only 6^3 will have a final digit of 6.

PROBLEM 39   If exactly 3 darts hit this target, how many different scores are possible?

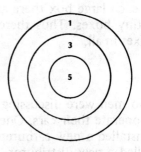

Figure B-3

Discussion   Make an exhaustive list:

5's	3's	1's	Score
3	0	0	15
2	1	0	13
2	0	1	11
1	2	0	11
1	1	1	9
1	0	2	7
0	3	0	9
0	2	1	7
0	1	2	5
0	0	3	3

Although there are 10 possibilities, there are two scores of 9, two scores of 7, and two scores of 11. Thus, only 7 scores are possible.

PROBLEM 40 A man owns one-half of a business. He sells one-fourth of his holdings for $12,500. What was the value of the business?

Discussion Work backwards. One-fourth of his share was $12,500. Thus his share is 4 times as much, or $50,000. Since he owned one-half of the business, it was worth twice as much, or $100,000.

PROBLEM 41 Della saves boxes. She puts them inside of each other to save room. She has 5 large boxes. Inside each of these, she puts 2 middle-sized boxes. Inside each middle-sized box she puts 5 tiny boxes. How many boxes does Della have in all?

Discussion Work the problem using one large box, and multiply by 5. In each large box there are 2 smaller boxes, each containing 5 tiny boxes. Thus there are 13 in this pile. 13 × 5 = 65 boxes in all.

PROBLEM 42 Two men were discussing how much they spent for gasoline to operate their cars. One told the other, "You know, Fred, I installed a new carburetor, and it saved me 36%. I then installed a new distributor, and it saved me 42%. I put on a set of new radial tires, and they saved me 53%. The mechanic tuned up the car and saved me 66%." Fred asked, "Now what happens?" "Well," said the first man, "whenever I drive anywhere, the car overflows!" What is your reaction to this story?

Discussion We have

Percentage of gasoline used before "improvements"	100
Percentage of gasoline used with new carburetor	$100 - 36 = 64$
Percentage of gasoline used with new distributor	$64 - .42(64) = 37.12$
Percentage of gasoline used with new tires	$37.12 - .53(37.12) = 17.45$
Percentage of gasoline used after tuneup	$17.45 - .66(17.45) = 5.93 \approx 6$

Thus, a trip that used to require 100 gallons of gasoline before any improvements were made would now take about 6 gallons of gasoline, a rather "tall" story.

PROBLEM 43　Jeff and Mike bred tropical fish. Mike decided to abandon the hobby and give his fish away. First he gave half of them and half a fish more to Scott. Then he gave half of what was left and half a fish more to Billy. That left Mike with only 1 fish, which he gave to Jeff. How many fish did Mike start with?

Discussion　Although we can solve this problem algebraically, the equation formed is rather complicated:

$$x - \left(\frac{x}{2} + \frac{1}{2}\right) - \left[\frac{x - \left(\frac{x}{2} + \frac{1}{2}\right)}{2} + \frac{1}{2}\right] = 1$$

If we work backwards (and assume that Mike doesn't cut any fish in half), we realize that we are working with a set of odd numbers. Since only 1 fish remained after Mike's last gift, he must have had 3 fish before giving the 1 to Jeff (half of 3, or 1½, plus ½ equals 2). So his gift to Billy was 2 fish. Working backwards in a similar manner, we find that Mike must have started with 7 fish and given 3½ + ½ (or 4) to Scott.

PROBLEM 44　Raffle tickets sell for $2.00 each. First prize is $1000 and second prize is $500. There are 6 third prizes of $100 each and 6 fourth prizes of $50 each. They made a profit of $600 on the raffle. How many tickets did they sell?

Discussion　To do this multi-stage problem, we first find the total value of the prizes ($2400). Add the profit ($600) and divide by $2.00. The result is 1500 tickets.

PROBLEM 45　What is the date when the month of February is 15,000 minutes old?

Discussion　There are 24 X 60 or 1,440 minutes in a day. Thus 15,000 ÷ 1440 = 10 + a remainder. The date is February 11th.

PROBLEM 46　When I arrange the members of a marching band in rows of 2, 3, or 4, there is always 1 person left over. However, when I arrange them in rows of 5, the rows are all even. What is the minimum number of people in the marching band?

Discussion　The number has the property that it always leaves a remainder of 1 when divided by 2, 3, or 4. The smallest number with this property is the LCM of 2, 3, and 4 with 1 added. The LCM of these numbers is 12; adding 1 we get 13. Thus the sequence that satisfies the requirements of the problem is 13, 25, 37, 49, 61, 73, 85, ... We know that the number is evenly divisible by 5, so the only possible answers at this point are 25 and 85. The minimum number is 25.

PROBLEM 47   If a brick balances with three-quarters of a brick plus three-quarters of a pound, then how much does the brick weigh?

Discussion   The three-quarters-of-a-pound weight must exactly balance the missing one-fourth of a brick. Thus 1/4 of a brick = 3/4 of a pound, and 4/4 of a brick = 4 times 3/4 of a pound, or 3 pounds.

PROBLEM 48   A textbook is opened at random. To what pages is it opened if the product of the facing page numbers is 3,192?

Discussion   Students can try pairs of successive numbers on their calculators until they find the product 3,192. An alternative method is to take the square root of 3,192. This gives 56.497787. Students then try the integers surrounding this number, namely 56 and 57.

PROBLEM 49   A senior class consists of 250 students, 40 percent of them girls. One half of the boys went on the class trip. How many boys stayed home?

Discussion   The key to this problem lies in the question being asked. A careful analysis of the given information is required. Since the question concerns "boys," we must translate the 40 percent who are girls into the 60 percent who are the boys.

PROBLEM 50   A pail with 40 washers in it weighs 175 grams. The same pail with 20 washers in it weighs 95 grams. How much does the pail weigh alone? How much does each washer weigh?

Discussion   Students can actually guess until they arrive at the answer (washers weigh 4 grams; the pail weighs 15 grams). Other students might reason in the following manner:

$$
\begin{array}{lr}
1 \text{ pail } + 20 \text{ washers} = & 95 \text{ grams} \\
\text{then } 2 \text{ pails} + 40 \text{ washers} = & 190 \text{ grams} \\
\underline{\text{but } 1 \text{ pail } + 40 \text{ washers} = 175 \text{ grams}} \\
1 \text{ pail } \qquad\qquad\quad = & 15 \text{ grams}
\end{array}
$$

$$1 \text{ pail } + 40 \text{ washers} = 175 \text{ grams}$$
$$\underline{1 \text{ pail } + 20 \text{ washers} = 95 \text{ grams}}$$
$$20 \text{ washers} = 80 \text{ grams}$$
$$1 \text{ washer } = 4 \text{ grams}$$

PROBLEM 51 The following advertisement appeared in the real estate section of a local newspaper:

INVEST FOR THE FUTURE!
LAND FOR SALE—
ONLY 5¢ PER SQUARE INCH!!

Invest your money now in land,
in an area that is soon to be developed.
For information, call or write

Land Developers, Inc.

If you were to buy an acre of land as advertised, what amount would you be required to pay?

Discussion In addition to teaching "number explosions," this problem introduces the topic of advertising and come-on programs. Mathematically it is an interesting problem for use with the calculator. The only information required is that an acre is 200' x 200'. Thus

$$(200 \times 12)(200 \times 12)(.05) = \$288{,}000 \text{ an acre}$$

PROBLEM 52 Mrs. Watkins buys candy at 80¢ a pound and sells it at 20¢ for a 2-ounce package. She sells 64 packages. What is her profit?

Discussion A 2-ounce package is 1/8 of a pound. This costs her 10¢. Thus she makes 10¢ on each package she sells. Her profit is 64 X 10¢ or $6.40.

PROBLEM 53 You have 9 cubes. You make four piles so that the first pile contains 3 more cubes than the second pile; the second pile contains one cube less than the third pile; the fourth pile contains twice as many cubes as the second pile. How many cubes are in each pile?

Discussion This is an excellent problem to be done by an experiment. Provide the students with a set of 9 cubes. By moving them about, the students arrive at the answer 4-1-2-2.

111

PROBLEM 54   A flag has 4 horizontal stripes. Green is on top, white and gold are not together, and white is between green and blue. What color stripe is on the bottom?

Discussion   By making a drawing and placing the colors according to the given conditions, we find that gold is the color of the bottom stripe.

PROBLEM 55   August 27th falls on a Tuesday. What are the dates of each Saturday in August?

Discussion   If August 27 is a Tuesday, then August 24 is a Saturday. Adding and subtracting 7's, we find that the dates of the Saturdays are August 3, 10, 17, 24, 31.

PROBLEM 56   Two clocks each show 12:00. One of the clocks runs backwards at the correct speed, while the other runs properly. When will they both next show the same time?

Discussion   Make a table:

CLOCK #1	12	11	10	9	8	7	6
CLOCK #2	12	1	2	3	4	5	6

They both show the same time at 6:00.

PROBLEM 57   The ratio of boys to girls on the camp volleyball team is 3 to 2. There are 4 more boys than girls on the team. How many girls are on the team?

Discussion   Guess and test! Make a list to keep track of the guesses. The answer, 8 girls, is easily found.

PROBLEM 58   Rose, Sally, and Tina are salespersons at a used car dealership. They sold a Ford, a Chevy, and a Plymouth. Rose and the person who sold the Ford are cousins. The person who sold the Chevy is older than Sally. Tina sold the Plymouth. Which car was sold by each woman?

Discussion   Prepare a 3 X 3 matrix to organize the data given by the clues. Tina sold the Plymouth, Rose sold the Chevy, and Sally sold the Ford.

PROBLEM 59   A farmer has a plot of land in the shape of a rectangle that is 32 feet long by 24 feet wide. He wishes to put a fence around the plot of land. If fence posts are to be placed every 8 feet, how many fence posts will he use?

Discussion   If we draw a picture of the field, we notice that the posts placed in the four corners need not be counted twice, even though they can be considered to be on two sides. Thus the farmer needs 14 posts, not the 18 that many students will give as their answer.

PROBLEM 60   A can filled with fruit juice weighs 20 ounces. When one-half of the juice is spilled out, the can and the remaining juice weigh 11½ ounces. How much did the can weigh?

Discussion   The weight of the juice that was spilled out was 20 − 11½ = 8½ ounces. Since this was one-half of the total weight of the juice, the juice must weigh 17 ounces. Thus the can weighs 3 ounces.

PROBLEM 61   A ball drops from a height of 96 feet and rebounds one-half of the total distance it has just fallen each time it bounces. What is the total distance it has traveled when it hits the ground the third time?

Discussion   Make a drawing to show the path of the ball. The distance it covers is 96 + 48 + 48 + 24 + 24 = 240 feet.

PROBLEM 62   On my birthday, I will be a multiple of 6 years old. Next year, I will be a multiple of 5 years old. I am older than 15 but younger than 40. How old am I?

Discussion   List the multiples of 6 that lie between 15 and 40: 18, 24, 30, 36. Only 24 will be a multiple of 5 in one year.

PROBLEM 63   On my birthday, I will be a multiple of 6 years old. Next year I will be a prime number of years old. If I am older than 15 but younger than 40, how old am I?

Discussion   List the multiples of 6 that lie between 15 and 40: 18, 24, 30, 36. This time, there are 3 numbers that will be primes when you add 1: 19, 31, 37. Thus this problem does not have one definite answer. Consider extending this problem to the first ten multiples of 6.

PROBLEM 64   Josh's dog got stuck on a ladder. When Josh tried to rescue him, the dog got scared and jumped 3 rungs further up. So, Josh stepped down. The dog lost his grip and slipped down 6 rungs to the 3rd rung on the ladder. From there, Josh picked up the dog. On what rung was the dog originally stuck?

Discussion   Make a drawing. The dog was originally stuck on the sixth rung of the ladder.

113

PROBLEM 65   To hang a picture on a bulletin board, Jim uses 4 thumbtacks, one in each corner. If he overlaps the corners, Jim can hang two pictures with only 6 tacks. What is the minimum number of tacks Jim needs to hang 6 pictures?

Discussion   A drawing will reveal that 2 rows of 3 pictures each is the most efficient way to hang 6 pictures. It will take only 12 tacks to do this.

PROBLEM 66   Lauren, Lois, and Nancy are going to earn some money by shoveling snow from people's walks. They will charge $7.50 per walk, and share the money equally. How much did Lois earn?

Discussion   Although the problem gives some numerical data, the number of walks they shovel is not given. Thus there is insufficient data to solve the problem. It is appropriate at times to give problems that have no answer. Ask the students to supply data so that an answer can be obtained.

PROBLEM 67   Mike has 15 coins that total $1.00. What are the coins and how many of each does he have?

Discussion   Guess and test with a table to record the data that will reveal one solution of 13 nickels, 1 dime, and 1 quarter.

*PROBLEM 68   All of the boxes in the figures are congruent squares. The first figure contains 5 squares and has an area of 20 square inches. The second figure is composed of 9 squares. What is its perimeter?

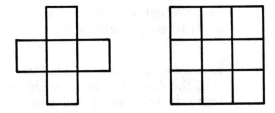

Figure B-4

Discussion   The first figure has an area of 20 square inches. Thus each square is 4 square inches, with a side of 2 inches. The second figure has a perimeter of 12 sides, or 24 inches.

*PROBLEM 69   The average of three fractions is 1. Two of the fractions are 1/3 and 1/4. What is the third fraction?

Discussion   For the average of the fractions to be 1, their sum must be 3. Find the sum of 1/3 + 1/4 and subtract from 3.

$$\frac{1}{3} + \frac{1}{4} = \frac{7}{12}$$

$$3 - \frac{7}{12} = \frac{29}{12}$$

*PROBLEM 70   A square piece of paper is folded in half and cut along the dotted line (the fold), as shown, to form 2 congruent rectangles. If the perimeter of each rectangle is 30 inches, what was the perimeter of the original piece of paper?

Figure B-5

Discussion   Let each side of the original square piece of paper be represented by $2s$. Then the perimeter of one rectangle is $s + s + 2s + 2s = 6s$. Since $6s = 30$, $s = 5$. Thus the original square had a perimeter of $8s$, or 40 inches.

PROBLEM 71   Two girls, Jan and Tanya, have a job painting fence posts that line both sides of a road leading to a barn. Jan arrived early and had already painted 5 posts when Tanya arrived. Before she started painting, Tanya said, "Jan, I'm left-handed and it's easier for me to paint this side of the road while you paint the other side." Jan agreed and went over to the other side of the road. Tanya painted all the posts on her side, then went across the road and painted 10 posts on Jan's side. This finished the job. If there were the same number of posts on each side of the road, who painted more posts and how many more?

Discussion   Tanya painted 10 posts from Jan's side, plus her own row minus the 5 Jan had already done. Thus Tanya painted an entire row plus 5 posts, while Jan painted an entire row minus 5. Tanya painted 10 more posts than Jan.

PROBLEM 72   In how many different ways can three people divide 25 pieces of candy so that each person gets at least 1 piece?

Discussion   We have

    3 pieces of candy: 1-1-1
    4 pieces of candy: 1-1-2; 1-2-1; 2-1-1
    5 pieces of candy: 1-1-3; 1-3-1; 3-1-1; 2-2-1; 2-1-2; 1-2-2

Prepare a chart.

Number of pieces of candy	3	4	5	6	7	...	n
Number of ways to distribute	1	3	6	10	15		$\dfrac{(n-1)(n-2)}{2}$

Thus, for 25 pieces of candy,

$$\frac{(24)\,(23)}{2} = 12 \times 23$$

$$= 276$$

There are 276 ways to distribute the pieces of candy.

PROBLEM 73   Two girls wish to find the speed of a moving freight train as it passes by their town. They find that 42 railroad cars pass by the corner in 1 minute. The average length of a railroad car is 60 feet. At what speed is the train moving in miles per hour?

Discussion   If 42 railroad cars pass by the corner in 1 minute, then 60 X 42 or 2,520 cars pass by in one hour. This is a total length of 2,520 X 60 or 151,200 feet per hour. Dividing this by 5,280 we obtain 28.6363. Thus the speed of the train is approximately 29 miles per hour. (Again, use of the calculator enables the problem-solving aspect to be emphasized.)

PROBLEM 74   I am a proper fraction. The sum of my numerator and my denominator is 1 less than a perfect square. Their difference is 1 more than a perfect square. Their product is 1 less than a perfect square. What fraction am I?

Discussion   Examine those products that are 1 less than a perfect square.

Perfect square minus 1	Possible product	Sum	Difference
0	–	–	–
3	1 X 3	4	2
8	1 X 8	9	7
8	2 X 4	6	2
15	1 X 15	16	14
15	3 X 5	8	2

Thus one answer to the problem is the fraction 3/5.

*PROBLEM 75   A cube that is 3 inches on each edge is painted completely red on all 6 faces. The cube is then cut into 27 smaller cubes, each measuring 1 inch on each edge. Of these 27 smaller cubes, how many have exactly 3 faces painted red? How many have exactly 2 faces painted red? How many have exactly 1 face painted red? How many have no faces painted red?

Discussion   Examine the diagram in Figure B–6. We can see that each of the 8 corner pieces will have exactly 3 faces painted red; the center piece on each face will have exactly 1 painted surface (there are 6 of these); the single cube in the exact center of the original cube will have no painted faces. There will be exactly 12 small cubes having paint on exactly 2 faces (numbered 1, 2, 3, . . . in the diagram).

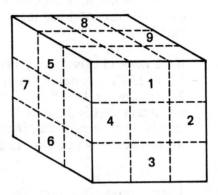

Figure B–6

PROBLEM 76   A father decided to divide $1200 among his four children in the following manner: each child would receive $100 more than the child who was next younger. How much does the oldest child receive?

Discussion   Guess and test. For those children who have an algebra background, this problem can be solved by using the equation

$$X + (X + 100) + (X + 200) + (X + 300) = 1200$$

PROBLEM 77   An oil storage tank recorded 1/12 full when its supply was replenished. After filling it, the tank recorded 7/8 full. If 1197 gallons were delivered, how many gallons of oil were in the tank before the delivery?

Discussion   Since the tank was 7/8 full at the end, and 1/12 full at the beginning, their difference, 19/24, represents the part of the tank that was filled with 1197 gallons. Dividing by 19, we find that there are 63 gallons per 24th, or 126 gallons in 1/12 of a tank. An alternate method would be to first determine the capacity of the full tank. This is done by multiplying 1,197 by 24/19.

PROBLEM 78   The probability of rolling a 2 on a standard pair of dice is 1/36; the probability of rolling a 3 is 2/36 (a 1-2 or a 2-1); and so on. How could you re-mark a pair of dice so that the probability of throwing each number from 1 through 12 was the same?

Discussion   If the probability of throwing each number from 1 through 12 is to be the same, then each must have a probability of 3/36. To allow you to roll a 1, the pair of dice would have to be marked with a 1 and a 0. To obtain the required prob-

118

ability of 3/36, there must be 3 such situations. Thus the results should be

Die 1	Die 2
0, 1, 2	1, 1, 1
3, 4, 5	7, 7, 7

PROBLEM 79

During the recent census, a man told the census-taker that he had three children. When asked their ages, he replied, "The product of their ages is 72. The sum of their ages is the same as my house number." The census-taker ran to the door and looked at the house number. "I still can't tell," she complained. The man replied, "Oh, that's right. I forgot to tell you that the oldest one likes chocolate pudding." The census-taker promptly wrote down the ages of the three children. How old are they?

Discussion

List all the combinations of three numbers whose product is 72, together with their sums:

1-1-72 = 74	2-2-18 = 22	3-3-8 = 14
1-2-36 = 39	2-3-12 = 17	3-4-6 = 13
1-3-24 = 28	2-4- 9 = 15	
1-4-18 = 23	2-6- 6 = 14	
1-6-12 = 19		
1-8- 9 = 18		

Since there was still a question after seeing the sum of the ages (the house number), there had to be more than one set of factors whose sum equaled this number (3-3-8 and 2-6-6). Since 2-6-6 does not yield an "oldest child" but 3-3-8 does, the ages of the children must have been 3, 3, and 8.

PROBLEM 80

The sum of two numbers is 2, and the product of these same numbers is 3. Find the sum of their reciprocals.

Discussion

The usual algebraic solution to this problem is as follows: Let x and y represent the two numbers. Then

$$x + y = 2$$
$$xy = 3$$

This yields a solution set

$$\begin{Bmatrix} x/x = 1 + i\sqrt{2} \\ y/y = 1 - i\sqrt{2} \end{Bmatrix}$$

Now we must sum the reciprocals:

$$\frac{1}{1 + i\sqrt{2}} + \frac{1}{1 - i\sqrt{2}} = \frac{(1 - i\sqrt{2}) + (1 + i\sqrt{2})}{(1 + i\sqrt{2})(1 - i\sqrt{2})} = \frac{2}{3}$$

119

However, there is a more artistic solution. The sum of the reciprocals of x and y is given by the expression

$$\frac{1}{x} + \frac{1}{y} = \frac{x+y}{xy} = \frac{2}{3}$$

PROBLEM 81   A bridge that spans a bay is 1 mile long and is suspended from two supports, one at each end. As a result, when it expands a total of 2 feet from the summer heat, it "buckles" in the center, causing a bulge. How high is the bulge?

Discussion   Draw a diagram of the bridge, both before and after the expansion causes it to buckle. (See Figure B–7.)

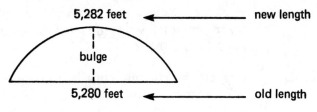

Figure B–7

We can now approximate the situation, using a diagram with two right triangles, as in Figure B–8.

Figure B–8

The Pythagorean Theorem can now be applied to the right triangle:

$$x^2 + (2,640)^2 = (2,641)^2$$
$$x^2 + 6,969,600 = 6,974,881$$
$$x^2 = 5,281$$
$$x = 72.67$$

Thus the bulge is approximately 73 feet high.

PROBLEM 82   A map of a local town is shown in Figure B–9. Billy lives at the corner of 4th Street and Fairfield Avenue. Betty lives at the corner of 8th Street and Appleton Avenue. Billy decides that he will visit Betty once a day after school until he has tried every different route to her house. Billy agrees to travel only east and north. How many different routes can Billy take to get to Betty's house?

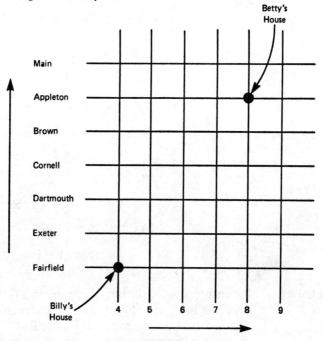

Figure B-9

Discussion The first attempts by students to solve this problem usually involve trying to draw and count all of the different routes. This procedure is extremely cumbersome. It is easier to consider the number of different routes to each point on the grid in Figure B-10.

Figure B-10

121

Notice that the numbers on the grid from the Pascal Triangle in Figure B-11

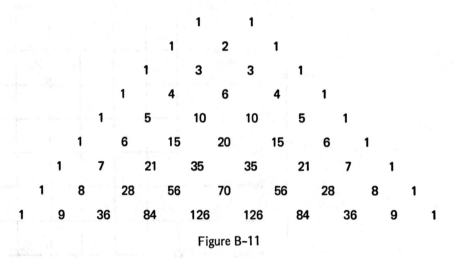

```
                    1        1
                1        2        1
            1        3        3        1
        1        4        6        4        1
    1        5       10       10        5        1
1        6       15       20       15        6        1
    1        7       21       35       35       21        7        1
        1        8       28       56       70       56       28        8        1
    1        9       36       84      126      126       84       36        9        1
```

Figure B-11

*PROBLEM 83   An interesting variation on problem 36 is the following. Suppose we limit the direction of movement along the streets to that shown by the arrows in Figure B-12. How many different routes are there now from point *A* to point *L*?

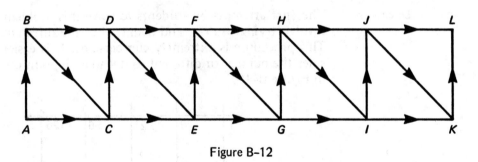

Figure B-12

Discussion   If we again examine the number of possible routes to each of the different points on the grid, we find another interesting series of numbers. (See Figure B-13.)

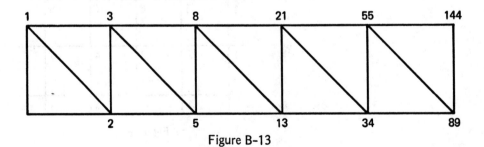

Figure B-13

122

The series 1, 2, 3, 5, 8, 13, 21, 34, 55, 89, 144, . . . is the Fibonacci sequence of numbers—that is, each term after the first two is derived by adding the preceding two terms of the series. There are 144 different routes from A to L.

*PROBLEM 84

A steel band is fitted tightly around the equator. The band is removed and cut, and an additional 10 feet is added. The band now fits more loosely than it did before. How high off the ground is the band?

Discussion

Reduce the problem to that of a circle of radius r. Thus its circumference is represented by $2\pi r$. Now, when we increase

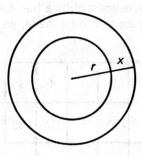

Figure B-14

the circumference by 10 feet, we increase the radius of the steel band by x. (See Figure B-14.) Thus,

$$2\pi(r + x) = 2\pi r + 10$$
$$2\pi r + 2\pi x = 2\pi r + 10$$
$$2\pi x = 10$$
$$x = \frac{10}{2\pi}$$

Therefore the steel band now fits approximately 1.6 feet above the surface of the earth.

PROBLEM 85

A tugboat is delivering 6,000 barrels of oil according to the following schedule: half of the barrels are dropped off at the first stop; half of the remaining barrels are dropped off at the second stop; half of the remaining barrels are dropped off at the third stop. If this pattern continues, at which stop will they drop off the last barrel of oil?

Discussion

Make a table:

Stops	0	1	2	3	4	5	6	7	8	9	10	11	12	13	14
Dropped off	0	3000	1500	750	375	187	94	47	23	12	6	3	1	1	1
Barrels remaining	6000	3000	1500	750	375	188	94	47	24	12	6	3	2	1	0

Table B-1

The final barrel of oil is dropped off at the 14th stop. Note that a decision has to be made at stop 5. Half of 375 is 187½. In this first case, we rounded *down* and continued this way whenever a choice had to be made. If we round *up* when the choice has to be made, we obtain a different table:

Stops	0	1	2	3	4	5	6	7	8	9	10	11	12	13
Dropped off	0	3000	1500	750	375	188	94	47	23	12	6	3	1	1
Barrels remaining	6000	3000	1500	750	375	187	93	46	23	11	5	2	1	0

Table B-2

Now the final barrel of oil is dropped off at the 13th stop.

PROBLEM 86   Find the value of

$$\frac{\sin 10° \quad \cos 10° \quad \tan 10° \quad \csc 10° \quad \sec 10° \quad \cot 10°}{\sin 20° \quad \cos 20° \quad \tan 20° \quad \csc 20° \quad \sec 20° \quad \cot 20°}$$

Discussion   Some students will go directly to the tables for the values of these functions. Others will use a calculator. A more elegant method of solution is to realize that $\sin x° \csc x° = 1$, $\cos x° \sec x° = 1$, and $\tan x° \cot x° = 1$. Thus the fraction reduces to 1/1 or simply 1.

PROBLEM 87   A cake in the form of a cube falls into a large vat of frosting and comes out frosted on all 6 faces. The cake is then cut into smaller cubes, each 1 inch on an edge. The cake is cut so that the number of pieces with frosting on 3 faces will be

1/8 the number of pieces having no frosting at all. We wish to have exactly enough pieces of cake for everyone. How many people will receive pieces of cake with frosting on exactly 3 faces? On exactly 2 faces? On exactly 1 face? On no faces? How large was the original cake?

Discussion

Make a table for a cube cake that originally was a $2 \times 2 \times 2$ cake, a $3 \times 3 \times 3$ cake, etc. Look for a pattern.

Cube	3 frosted faces	2 frosted faces	1 frosted faces	0 frosted faces	
$2 \times 2 \times 2$	8	0	0	0	= 8
$3 \times 3 \times 3$	8	12	6	1	= 27
$4 \times 4 \times 4$	8	24	24	8	= 64
$5 \times 5 \times 5$	8	36	54	27	= 125
$6 \times 6 \times 6$	8	48	96	64	= 216

Notice that the number of small cubes with exactly 3 frosted faces is *always* 8. Thus the cube we are looking for is the cube having 8 times as many no-frosting faces, or 64. This is the $6 \times 6 \times 6$ cube, as shown on our chart. Thus there are 48 cubes with frosting on exactly 2 faces, 96 cubes with frosting on exactly 1 face, and a total of 216 small cubes in all. The original cake must have been a $6 \times 6 \times 6$ cube.

PROBLEM 88

A commuter is in the habit of arriving at his suburban station each evening at exactly 6:00 P.M. His wife is always waiting for him with the car; she too arrives at exactly 6:00 P.M. She never varies her route or her rate of speed. One day he takes an earlier train, arriving at the station at 5:00 P.M. He decides not to call his wife, but begins to walk toward home along the route she always takes. They meet somewhere along the route, he gets into the car, and they drive home. They arrive home 10 minutes earlier than usual. How long had the husband been walking when he was picked up by his wife?

Discussion

If we pursue the problem from the point of view of the husband's time, we cannot arrive at an answer easily. So consider the problem from the point of view of the wife—i.e., how long she is gone from the house. Since they arrive home a total of 10 minutes earlier than usual, the car was gone a total of 5 minutes less in each direction. Thus the husband had been walking a total of 55 minutes when he was picked up.

PROBLEM 89   A woman was 3/8 of the way across a bridge when she heard the Wabash Cannonball Express approaching the bridge at 60 miles per hour. She quickly calculated that she could *just* save herself by running to either end of the bridge at top speed. How fast could she run?

Discussion   Draw a diagram, as in Figure B–15. We see that there are two different situations to consider.

Figure B–15

If she can just get to either end of the bridge before the train arrives at that end, let her run away from the train toward point *B*. When the train arrives at point *A*, she will have covered an additional 3/8 of the bridge's length, or 3/4 of the bridge. She can now run the remaining 1/4 in the same time it will take the train to cover the entire 4/4 of the bridge. Thus her rate is 1/4 of that of the train, or 15 miles per hour.

Notice that a more formal algebraic solution can also be used. Let the bridge be 8 units of length, for example. Let *x* represent the distance the train is from point *A*; let *y* represent the woman's rate. Then we obtain the following two equations:

$$\frac{3}{y} = \frac{x}{60} \text{ (if the woman runs toward point } A)$$

$$\frac{5}{y} = \frac{x+8}{60} \text{ (if the woman runs toward point } B)$$

from which we get $y = 15$.

PROBLEM 90   Using the digits 1, 2, 3, 4, what is the largest product of two numbers that can be formed?

126

Discussion Guess and test each guess. Use a list to keep track of your guesses. Some examples might include 41 X 23 = 943, 14 X 32 = 448, 421 X 3 = 1263, etc. The largest product is 41 X 32 = 1312.

PROBLEM 91 Ed and Dave were walking when they saw three people coming toward them. "I wonder how old they are," said Ed. Dave replied, "I know them! The product of their ages is 2,450, and the sum of their ages is twice your age." "That's all well and good," said Ed, "but I need some more information." "Oh, ves," agreed Dave. "Well, I'm older than any of the three." "Now I can figure their ages," said Ed.

Discussion We need to look at all the combinations of three factors whose product is 2,450.

5-14-35 (sum 54)	5-10-49 (sum 64)
10-35- 7 (sum 52)	2-25-49 (sum 76)
5- 5-28 (sum 38)	7-14-25 (sum 46)
7- 7-50 (sum 64)	7- 5-70 (sum 82)

Notice that there are others, but the factors could not represent ages under normal circumstances (e.g., 1-2-1,225, 1-10-245, etc.). Since the information "I am older than any of the three" is needed to provide a unique solution, Dave must be 50. If he were 51 or older, then both solutions whose sum equals 64 would be possible. Hence he must be 50, and the solution must be 49-10-5.

PROBLEM 92 Two bicycle riders, Jeff and Nancy, are 25 miles apart, riding toward each other at speeds of 15 miles per hour and 10 miles per hour, respectively. A fly starts from Jeff and flies toward Nancy and then back to Jeff again and so on. The fly continues flying back and forth at a constant rate of 40 miles per hour, until the bicycle riders "collide" and crush the fly. How far has the fly traveled?

Discussion If we try to solve the problem using distance as our main focus, we arrive at a very complex series of equations. However, carefully examine the time it takes Jeff and Nancy to meet and crush the fly. Since they are moving toward each other at a constant rate of 25 miles per hour, it will take them only 1 hour of bicycling to reach each other. Thus the fly is moving back and forth for one hour, or a total of 40 miles.

127

PROBLEM 93 Two gentlemen were trying to decide when to open their store for business. "When the day after tomorrow is yesterday," said Marv, "then 'today' will be as far from Sunday as that day which was 'today' when the day before yesterday was tomorrow!" On which day of the week were the two men talking?

Discussion Diagramming the conversation will lead us to discover that the men were talking on Sunday.

PROBLEM 94 A baker rolls out his dough in the morning and cuts it into 8 equal pieces, which he seasons. He then cuts each of these seasoned pieces into 4 equal parts. He bakes each of these into a loaf of bread that is 3/4 of a foot long. If we were to place all of these loaves end-to-end, how long would the total length be?

Discussion Simulate the action with a drawing. The baker made 8 X 4 or 32 loaves, with each loaf 9 inches long. Thus the length would be 32 X 9" = 288" or 24 feet.

PROBLEM 95 If 3/4 of a number is added to 15, the result is twice the original number. What is the original number?

Discussion Guess and test, using a table to keep track of the guesses made. Notice that we confine our guesses to multiples of 4:

Number (N)	(3/4)N	Add 15	Result
4	3	18	Not 2 X 4
8	6	21	Not 2 X 8
12	9	24	24 = 2 X 12

The correct answer is 12.

PROBLEM 96 The factory planners have built stations for their night watchmen at points A and B in Figure B–16. They are now ready to install check-in boxes along the two intersecting walls RS and TU. They wish to install these check-in boxes so that the watchmen walking from station A to the box on RS to the box on TU to station B will be making a minimum trip. What is the shortest path meeting these conditions?

128

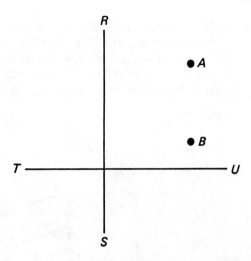

Figure B–16

Discussion This problem requires a double reflection. We first reflect *B* through *TU* to point *B'*. (See Figure B–17.) Then we reflect *B'* through *RS* to *B"*. Now we draw *AB"* to find the point for the check-in station along *RS* (point *C*). Then we draw *CB'* to find point *D* along *TU*.

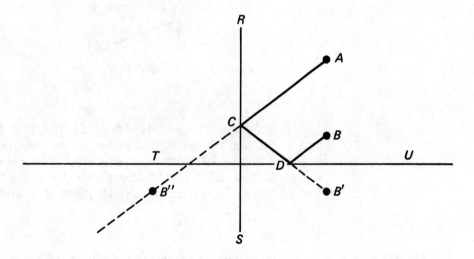

Figure B–17

PROBLEM 97 Lee must send one holiday gift out early this year. She doesn't know the exact amount of postage she will need to send it, but she does know it will be less than $3.19. She wants to buy as many stamps as necessary to make any combination up to $3.19. She could buy all 1¢ stamps, but that many might not fit on the package. What is the minimum number of stamps Lee should buy?

Discussion   We can take one-half the amount (rounding off to the next highest amount). This, together with stamps that make up the remaining one-half, will enable Lee to make any combination. We now repeat this procedure, always taking one-half the remainder. Thus we get Figure B–18.

Figure B–18

If Lee buys stamps of 1¢, 1¢, 2¢, 5¢, 10¢, 20¢, 40¢, 80¢, and $1.60, she will be able to make any combination up to and including $3.19. Notice that this is not a unique solution; she could buy other combinations also containing 9 stamps (for example, 1¢, 1¢, 2¢, 4¢, 9¢, 19¢, 39¢, 79¢, and $1.65).

PROBLEM 98   There are 16 football teams in the National Football League. To conduct their annual draft, teams in each city must have a direct telephone line to each of the other cities. How many direct telephone lines must be installed by the telephone company to accomplish this? Suppose the league expands to 24 teams?

Discussion   Examine the problem using smaller numbers. We can start the search for a pattern by using 1 city, 2 cities, 3 cities, etc. (See Figure B–19.)

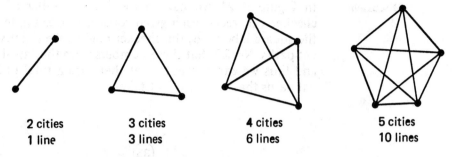

| | 2 cities | 3 cities | 4 cities | 5 cities |
| | 1 line | 3 lines | 6 lines | 10 lines |

Figure B-19

Number of cities	1	2	3	4	5	...	n
Number of lines	0	1	3	6	10	...	

Thus each city is connected to every other $(n-1)$ city. Since every 2 cities share a line, our total will be $\dfrac{n(n-1)}{2}$. For 16 teams the total will be $\dfrac{(16)(15)}{2}$ or 120 telephone lines. For 24 teams the total will be $\dfrac{(24)(23)}{2}$ or 276 lines.

*PROBLEM 99   The checkerboard shown in Figure B-20 contains one checker. The checker can only move diagonally "up" the board along the white squares. In how many ways can this checker reach the square marked A?

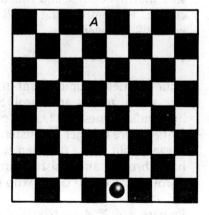

Figure B-20

131

Discussion

In Figure B-21 we have marked the number of ways the checker can reach each given square. For example, to reach the square labeled *B*, the checker might take exactly 3 different paths. Notice that these numbers form the Pascal Triangle, and thus we can compute that there are a total of 35 different paths the checker might take.

Figure B-21

PROBLEM 100

Two couples sitting on a park bench pose for a picture. If neither couple wishes to be separated, what is the number of different possible seating arrangements that can be used for the photograph?

Discussion

Simulate the action with a drawing. Let the letters *A*, *B* represent the first couple and the letters *C*, *D* represent the second couple. Remember that *A*, *B* is different from *B*, *A*. There will be 8 arrangements.

PROBLEM 101

Four married couples went to the baseball game last week. The wives' names are Carol, Sue, Jeanette, and Arlene. The husbands' names are Dan, Bob, Gary, and Frank. Bob and Jeanette are brother and sister. Jeanette and Frank were once engaged, but broke up when Jeanette met her husband. Arlene has a brother and a sister, but her husband is an only child. Carol is married to Gary. Who is married to whom?

Discussion

Prepare a 4 X 4 matrix like the one shown below. Use the clues to eliminate the incorrect choices.

132

	CAROL	SUE	JEANETTE	ARLENE
FRANK	✕	✕	✕	Yes
GARY	Yes	✕	✕	✕
BOB	✕	Yes	✕	✕
DAN	✕	✕	Yes	✕

PROBLEM 102　Mr. Lopez, who is 6 feet tall, wants to install a mirror on his bedroom wall that will enable him to see a full view of himself. What is the minimum-length mirror that will serve his needs, and how should it be placed on his wall?

Discussion　This interesting problem is resolved by applying a well-known theorem of geometry. A drawing, such as the one in Figure B-22, is the vital solution strategy.

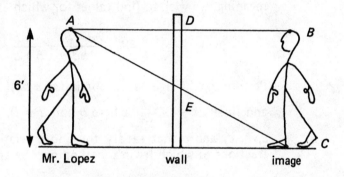

Figure B-22

Since the object, the image, and the wall are each perpendicular to the floor, the lines are parallel. Thus triangle *ABC* has segment *DE* parallel to *BC* and equal in length to half of *BC*. The conclusion is that the mirror must be 3 feet in length and hung so that its lower edge is 3 feet from the floor. Notice how Figure B-23 shows that the distance Mr. Lopez stands from the mirror does not affect the answer.

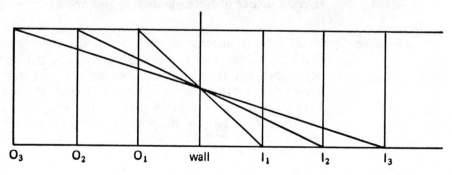

Figure B-23

PROBLEM 103   Irwin insists on adding two fractions by adding their numerators and then adding their denominators. Thus, when adding 9/12 and −1/4, Irwin gets

$$\frac{9 + -1}{12 + \ 4} = \frac{8}{16} = \frac{1}{2}$$

To show his method is correct, Irwin adds 9/12 and −1/4 in the usual manner and gets

$$\frac{9 + -3}{12} = \frac{6}{12} = \frac{1}{2}$$

Are there other values for which $\dfrac{a}{b} + \dfrac{c}{d} = \dfrac{a+c}{b+d}$?

Discussion   Since $\dfrac{a}{b} + \dfrac{c}{d} = \dfrac{a+c}{b+d}$ merely adds symbols with no regard for meaning, we wish to find values for which

$$\frac{a}{b} + \frac{c}{d} = \frac{ad + bc}{bd} = \frac{a+c}{b+d}$$

Performing the algebra, we obtain $(ad + bc)(b + d) = bd(a + c)$, and finally $c = -\dfrac{ad^2}{b^2}$, where b and $d \neq 0$. Integral values of a, b, c, and d that satisfy the above relationship will yield fractions to which Irwin's method may be applied.

PROBLEM 104   The Appletree Garden Service must plant 69,489 apple trees in the 9 days before winter sets in. Every day after the first, the foreman puts 6 additional men on the job. However, every day after the first, each man plants 5 fewer trees than each did on the previous day. As a result, the number of trees planted per man keeps going down each day. What was the largest number of trees planted on any one day?

Discussion   If we let the number of men working on the middle (the fifth) day be m, and the number of trees planted on that day be n, then mn trees were planted on the fifth day. On the fourth day, there were $(m − 6)(n + 5)$ trees planted; on the sixth day, there were $(m + 6)(n − 5)$ trees planted; and so on. Thus the totals for the 9 days would be $9mn − 1{,}800 = 69{,}489$, or $mn = 7{,}921$. Now 7,921 is the square of 89 (a prime number). Hence the chart of the work done would be

Day 1	65 men × 109 trees	= 7,085
Day 2	71 men × 104 trees	= 7,384
Day 3	77 men × 99 trees	= 7,623
Day 4	83 men × 94 trees	= 7,802
Day 5	89 men × 89 trees	= 7,921
Day 6	95 men × 84 trees	= 7,980
Day 7	101 men × 79 trees	= 7,979
Day 8	107 men × 74 trees	= 7,918
Day 9	113 men × 69 trees	= 7,797
		69,489

The largest number of trees planted on any one day was 7,980 trees on the sixth day.

PROBLEM 105

In a game called crossball, a team can score either 3 points or 7 points. Which scores can a team *not* make?

Discussion

We set up a table to organize our discussion:

Not possible	1	2		4	5			8			11					
Possible			3			6	7		9	10		12	13	14	15	...

Apparently a team can make every score after 11.

Notice that we can extend this problem as follows: Given any two relatively prime numbers, what is the greatest counting number that cannot be expressed using these numbers either singly, repeatedly, in addition, or in combination? (This leads to the formula $ab - (a + b)$ as the method for determining the answer.)

PROBLEM 106

Three cylindrical oil drums of 2-foot diameter are to be securely fastened in the form of a "triangle" by a steel band. What length of band will be required?

Discussion

The careful drawing of the situation in Figure B-24 is the fundamental strategy used here.

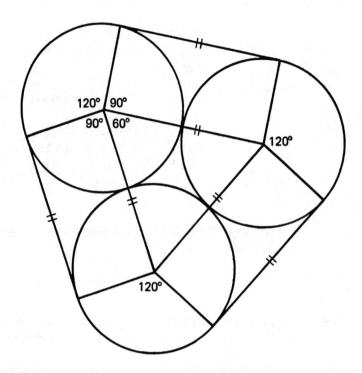

Figure B–24

Notice that the band consists of three straight sections (tangents) and three curved sections (arcs). The straight sections form rectangles with the line of centers, and thus each equals 2r or 2 feet. The curved sections are each arcs whose central angle is 120°, and thus each arc is 1/3 of a circle, or $(1/3)(\pi d)$. The total length is

$$3(2) + 3(\frac{1}{3}\pi d) = 6 + \pi d$$

Since $d = 2$ feet, the length of the steel band will be $6 + 2\pi$ feet, or approximately 12.28 feet.

Notice that this problem can be generalized for n barrels and also extended to barrels of different diameters.

PROBLEM 107   A meter records voltage readings between 0 and 20 volts. If the average value for the three readings on the meter was 16 volts, what could have been the smallest possible reading?

Discussion   If the average for three readings was 16, then the total for the three readings must have been 3 X 16 = 48. Since the reading can only be a maximum of 20, we use 2 X 20 = 40, leaving a minimum possible reading of 8 volts.

PROBLEM 108 A high school geometry class was given the problem of find-ing the height of the flagpole in the school yard with only a mirror and a measuring tape. Several of the students success-fully answered the question. How did they solve the problem?

Discussion Draw a diagram of the situation, as in Figure B–25.

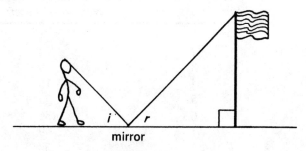

mirror

Figure B–25

Since the two triangles are similar (the angle of incidence *i* equals the angle of reflection *r*), a simple proportion reveals the answer.

PROBLEM 109 The shuttle service has a train going from New York to Boston and from Boston to New York, every hour on the hour. The trip from one city to the other takes 4½ hours. How many of the Boston to New York trains will pass you on your trip from New York to Boston if you leave New York at 9:00?

Discussion Simulate the action with a table:

Leaves Boston	Arrives New York
5:00	9:30
6:00	10:30
7:00	11:30
8:00	12:30
9:00	1:30
10:00	2:30
11:00	3:30
12:00	4:30
1:00	5:30

A total of 9 trains will pass you on the trip.

PROBLEM 110 Samantha wants to pile grapefruits in a store display in the form of a pyramid. She places 1 on the top layer, 4 in the

137

second layer, 9 in the third layer, 16 in the fourth layer, and so on. How many layers will she have if she uses all 385 grapefruits?

Discussion   Guess and test with a list to record the information.

Number of layers	Number of grapefruit	Total number
1	1	1
2	4	5
3	9	14
4	16	30
5	25	55
6	36	91
7	49	140
8	64	204
9	81	285
10	100	385

She will have a pyramid with 10 layers.

SECTION C

A Bibliography of Problem-Solving Resources

Adler, Irving. *Magic House of Numbers.* John Day Company, New York, New York, 1974.

Arithmetic Teacher. The entire November 1977 and February 1982 issues are devoted to problem solving. National Council of Teachers of Mathematics, Reston, Virginia.

Ball, W. W. R. *Mathematical Recreations and Essays* (12th edition, revised by H. S. M. Coxeter). Reprinted by University of Toronto Press, Toronto, Ontario, 1974.

Barnard, Douglas. *A Book of Mathematical and Reasoning Problems.* D. Van Nostrand Company, New York, New York, 1962.

Bransford, John D., and Stein, Barry S. *The Ideal Problem Solver.* W. H. Freeman and Co., San Francisco, California, 1984.

Butts, Thomas. *Problem Solving in Mathematics.* Scott, Foresman and Company, Glenview, Illinois, 1973.

Charosh, Mannis (editor). *Mathematical Challenges.* National Council of Teachers of Mathematics, Reston, Virginia, 1973.

Dodson, J. *Characteristics of Successful Insightful Problem Solvers.* University Microfilm, Number 71-13, 048, Ann Arbor, Michigan, 1970.

Dolan, Daniel T., and Williamson, James. *Teaching Problem Solving Strategies.* Addison-Wesley Publishing Company, Menlo Park, California, 1983.

Dudeney, H. E. *Amusements in Mathematics.* Dover Publishing Company, New York, New York, 1958.

Enrichment for the Grades, Twenty-seventh yearbook. National Council of Teachers of Mathematics, Reston, Virginia, 1966-1971.

Fixx, James. *Games for the Superintelligent.* Doubleday and Company, Garden City, New York, 1972.

Frolichstein, Jack. *Mathematical Fun, Games and Puzzles.* Dover Publishing Company, New York, New York, 1967.

Gardner, Martin. *Aha!* Scientific American/W. H. Freeman and Company, San Francisco, California, 1978.

_____. *Scientific American Book of Mathematical Puzzles and Diversions.* Simon and Schuster, New York, New York, 1959.

_____. *Second Scientific American Book of Mathematical Puzzles and Diversions.* Simon and Schuster, New York, New York, 1961.

_____ (editor). *Mathematic Puzzles of Sam Lloyd.* Simon and Schuster, New York, New York, 1959.

_____ (editor). *More Mathematical Puzzles of Sam Lloyd.* Simon and Schuster, New York, New York, 1960.

Greenes, Carole; Gregory, John; and Seymour, Dale. *Successful Problem Solving Techniques.* Creative Publications, Palo Alto, California, 1978.

_____; Spungin, Rika; and Dombrowski, Justine M. *Problem-Matics.* Creative Publications, Palo Alto, California, 1978.

Haynes, John R. *The Complete Problem Solver.* Franklin Institute Press, Philadelphia, Pennsylvania, 1981.

Heafford, Philip. *The Math Entertainer.* Harper & Row, Publishers, New York, New York, 1973.

Heafford, Philip. *The Math Entertainer.* Harper & Row, Publishers, New York, New York, 1973.

Jacoby, Oswald, and Benson, William H. *Mathematics for Pleasure.* Fawcett World Library, New York, New York, 1965.

Kaufman, Gerald L. *The Book of Modern Puzzles.* Dover Publishing Company, New York, New York, 1954.

Kordemsky, Boris A. *The Moscow Puzzles.* Charles Scribner's Sons, New York, New York, 1972.

Kraitchik, Maurice. *Mathematical Recreations* (2nd edition). Dover Publishing Company, New York, New York, 1953.

Krulik, Stephen, and Rudnick, Jesse A. *A Sourcebook for Teaching Problem Solving.* Allyn and Bacon, Inc., Newton, Massachusetts, 1984.

———. *Problem Solving in Math (G and H).* Scholastic Book Services, New York, New York, 1982.

Lenchner, George. *Creative Problem Solving in School Mathematics.* Houghton Mifflin, Inc., Boston, Massachusetts, 1983.

Longley-Cook, L. H. *New Math Puzzle Book.* Van Nostrand Reinhold Company, New York, New York, 1970.

May, Francis B. *Introduction to Games of Strategy.* Allyn and Bacon, Boston, Massachusetts, 1970.

Mira, Julio. *Mathematical Teasers.* Barnes and Noble, New York, New York, 1970.

Mott-Smith, Geoffrey. *Mathematical Puzzles for Beginners and Enthusiasts* (2nd edition). Dover Publishing Company, New York, New York, 1954.

Peck, Lyman. *Secret Codes, Remainder Arithmetic, and Matrices.* National Council of Teachers of Mathematics, Reston, Virginia, 1961.

Polya, George. *How to Solve It.* Princeton University Press, Princeton, New Jersey, 1971.

———. *Mathematical Discovery: On Understanding, Learning and Teaching Problem Solving* (two volumes). John Wiley and Sons, New York, New York (Volume 1) 1962, (Volume 2) 1965.

———, and Kilpatrick, Jeremy. *The Stanford Mathematics Problem Book.* Teachers College Press, New York, New York, 1974.

Problem Solving in School Mathematics. 1980 Yearbook of the National Council of Teachers of Mathematics, Reston, Virginia, 1980.

Problematical Recreations. A series of small pamphlets containing puzzles and problems. Litton Industries, Inc., Beverly Hills, California.

Rademacher, Hans, and Toeplitz, Otto. *The Enjoyment of Mathematics.* Princeton University Press, Princeton, New Jersey, 1957.

Ranucci, Ernest. *Puzzles, Problems, Posers, and Pastimes* (three volumes). Houghton Mifflin Company, Boston, Massachusetts, 1972.

Salkind, Charles T. *The Contest Problem Book* (two volumes). Mathematical Association of America, Washington, D.C., 1975.

Schaaf, William. *A Bibliography of Recreational Mathematics* (four volumes). National Council of Teachers of Mathematics, Reston, Virginia (Volume 1) 1970, (Volume 2) 1970, (Volume 3) 1973, (Volume 4) 1978.

School Science and Mathematics. The entire March 1978 issue is devoted to problem solving. School Science and Mathematics Association, Inc., Kalamazoo, Michigan.

Shklarsky, D. O.; Chentzov, N. N.; and Yaglom, I. M. *The U.S.S.R. Olympiad Problem Book.* W. H. Freeman and Company, San Francisco, California, 1962.

Trigg, C. W. *Mathematical Quickies.* McGraw-Hill Book Company, New York, New York, 1967.

Wickelgren, Wayne. *How to Solve Problems.* W. H. Freeman and Company, San Francisco, California, 1974.

Williams, J. D. *The Compleat Strategyst* (rev. ed.). McGraw-Hill Book Company, New York, New York, 1965.

Wylie, C. R. *One Hundred One Puzzles in Thought and Logic.* Dover Publishing Company, New York, New York, 1957.

SECTION D

Masters for
Selected Problems

The following problems are from Chapters 1, 2, and 3:

1. Locker problem on page 8
2. Handshake problem on page 9
3. Checkerboard problem on page 10
4. Card game problem on page 41
5. Scale problem on page 47
6. Pirate problem on page 55
7. Triangle problem on page 58
8. Hamburger problem on page 64
9. Billiard problem on page 72

The following problems are from Section B:

10. #3
11. #5
12. #9
13. #12
14. #13
15. #21
16. #22
17. #28
18. #33
19. #39
20. #41
21. #44
22. #45
23. #51
24. #72
25. #78
26. #79
27. #81
28. #82
29. #85
30. #87
31. #99
32. #101
33. #103
34. #109
35. #110

Problem: The new school has exactly 1,000 lockers and exactly 1,000 students. On the first day of school, the students meet outside the building and agree on the following plan: The first student will enter the school and open all of the lockers. The second student will then enter the school and close every locker with an even number (2, 4, 6, 8, . . .). The third student will then "reverse" every third locker. That is, if the locker is closed, he will open it; if the locker is open, he will close it. The fourth student will reverse every fourth locker, and so on until all 1,000 students in turn have entered the building and reversed the proper lockers. Which lockers will finally remain open?

Problem: There are eight people in a room. Each person shakes hands with each of the other people once and only once. How many handshakes are there?

Problem: How many squares are there on a standard checkerboard?

Problem: The 7 and 8 keys on my calculator don't work. How might I find the sum of 274 + 882 + 1,028?

Problem: A, B, and C decide to play a game of cards. They agree on the following procedure: When a player loses a game, he or she will double the amount of money that each of the other players already has. First A loses a hand and doubles the amount of money that B and C each have. Then B loses a hand and doubles the amount of money that A and C each have. Then C loses a hand and doubles the amount of money that A and B each have. The three players then decide to quit, and they find that each player now has $8. Who was the biggest loser?

Problem: Three boys stood on a scale and put a nickel in the slot. The scale showed 390 pounds as their total weight. One boy stepped off the scale. It then showed 255 pounds. The second boy stepped off the scale, and it then showed 145 pounds. Find the weights of all three boys.

Problem: A pirate ship at point A in the diagram shown is 50 meters directly north of point C on the shore. Point D, also on the shore and due east of point C, is 130 meters from point C. Point B, a lighthouse, is due north of point D and 80 meters from point D. The pirate ship must touch the shoreline and then sail to the lighthouse. Find the location of point X on the shoreline, so that the path from A to X to B will be a minimum.

Problem: How many triangles can you find in this figure?

Problem: A major hamburger chain has sold 22 billion hamburgers, each 1 inch thick. If we stacked these hamburgers, how many miles high would the stack be?

Problem: Three boxes each contain a number of billiard balls. One box contains only even-numbered billiard balls, one box contains only odd-numbered billiard balls, and the third box contains a mixture of odd- and even-numbered billiard balls. *All* of the boxes are mislabeled. By selecting one ball from one of the boxes, can you correctly label the three boxes? Why or why not?

Problem: What is the sum of the numbers in this table?

3/4	3/8	3/7	3/5	3/13
2/5	4/7	10/13	5/8	1/4

NAME _____ DATE _____

Problem: You are waiting for the elevator to take you to a restaurant on the 70th floor of the Hancock Building. There are 45 people in line ahead of you. If each elevator can carry 10 people, on which trip will you be?

Problem: A football team won 3 more games than it lost. The team played 11 games. How many games did they lose?

Problem: A woman has some cows and some chickens. Together the animals have a total of 54 legs. How many cows and how many chickens might she have?

Problem: What was the final score of the Tigers-Sharks baseball game?

       (a) The sum of their scores was 8.
       (b) The product of their scores was 15.
       (c) The Sharks won the game.

Problem: Luisa was playing darts. She threw 6 darts, and all 6 hit the target shown. Which of the following could be her score?

4, 17, 56, 28, 29, 31

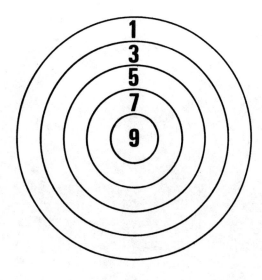

Problem: What's my number?

        (a) I am a two-digit number.
        (b) I am a multiple of 6.
        (c) The sum of my digits is 9.
        (d) My ten's digit is one-half of my unit's digit.

Problem: If a pound of plums contains 4 to 6 plums, what is the least possible weight in pounds of 3 dozen plums?

Problem: A merchant who was liquidating his stock offered various items at the following prices:

7 items at $10 per item
12 items at $ 8 per item
15 items at $ 6 per item
6 items at $ 5 per item.

If he sold one-half of this stock on the first day, what is the most money he could have received?

Problem: If exactly 3 darts hit this target, how many different scores are possible?

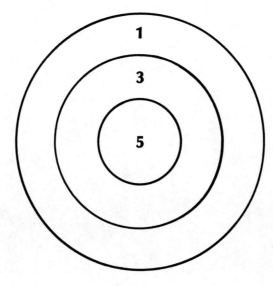

Problem: Della saves boxes. She puts them inside of each other to save room. She has 5 large boxes. Inside each of these, she puts 2 middle-sized boxes. Inside each middle-sized box she puts 5 tiny boxes. How many boxes does Della have in all?

Problem: Raffle tickets sell for $2.00 each. First prize is $1,000 and second prize is $500. There are 6 third prizes of $100 each and 6 fourth prizes of $50 each. They made a profit of $600 on the raffle. How many tickets did they sell?

Problem: What is the date when the month of February is 15,000 minutes old?

Problem: The following advertisement appeared in the real estate section of a local newspaper:

INVESTMENT FOR THE FUTURE!
LAND FOR SALE—
ONLY 5¢ PER SQUARE INCH!!

Invest your money now in land,
in an area that is soon to be developed.
For information, call or write

Land Developers, Inc.

If you were to buy an acre of land as advertised, what amount would you be required to pay?

Problem: In how many different ways can three people divide 25 pieces of candy so that each person gets at least 1 piece?

Problem: The probability of rolling a 2 on a standard pair of dice is 1/36; the probability of rolling a 3 is 2/36 (a 1-2 or a 2-1); and so on. How could you re-mark a pair of dice so that the probability of throwing each number from 1 through 12 was the same?

Problem: During the recent census, a man told the census-taker that he had three children. When asked their ages, he replied, "The product of their ages is 72. The sum of their ages is the same as my house number." The census-taker ran to the door and looked at the house number. "I still can't tell," she complained. The man replied, "Oh, that's right. I forgot to tell you that the oldest one likes chocolate pudding." The census-taker promptly wrote down the ages of the three children. How old are they?

Problem: A bridge that spans a bay is 1 mile long and is suspended from two supports, one at each end. As a result, when it expands a total of 2 feet from the summer heat, it "buckles" in the center, causing a bulge. How high is the bulge?

Problem: A map of a local town is shown in the figure below. Billy lives at the corner of 4th Street and Fairfield Avenue. Betty lives at the corner of 8th Street and Appleton Avenue. Billy decides that he will visit Betty once a day after school until he has tried every different route to her house. Billy agrees to travel only east and north. How many different routes can Billy take to get to Betty's house?

Problem: A tugboat is delivering 6,000 barrels of oil according to the following schedule: half of the barrels are dropped off at the first stop; half of the remaining barrels are dropped off at the second stop; half of the remaining barrels are dropped off at the third stop. If this pattern continues, at which stop will they drop off the last barrel of oil?

Problem: A cake in the form of a cube falls into a large vat of frosting and comes out frosted on all 6 faces. The cake is then cut into smaller cubes, each 1 inch on an edge. The cake is cut so that the number of pieces with frosting on 3 faces will be 1/8 the number of pieces having no frosting at all. We wish to have exactly enough pieces of cake for everyone. How many people will receive pieces of cake with frosting on exactly 3 faces? On exactly 2 faces? On exactly 1 face? On no faces? How large was the original cake?

Problem: The checkerboard shown in the figure contains one checker. The checker can only move diagonally "up" the board along the white squares. In how many ways can this checker reach the square marked A?

Problem: Four married couples went to the baseball game last week. The wives' names are Carol, Sue, Jeanette, and Arlene. The husbands' names are Dan, Bob, Gary, and Frank. Bob and Jeanette are brother and sister. Jeanette and Frank were once engaged, but broke up when Jeanette met her husband. Arlene has a brother and a sister, but her husband is an only child. Carol is married to Gary. Who is married to whom?

Problem: Irwin insists on adding two fractions by adding their numerators and then adding their denominators. Thus when adding 9/12 and −1/4, Irwin gets

$$\frac{9 + -1}{12 + 4} = \frac{8}{16} = \frac{1}{2}$$

To show that this is correct, Irwin adds 9/12 and −1/4 in the usual manner and gets

$$\frac{9 + -3}{12} = \frac{6}{12} = \frac{1}{2}$$

Are there any other values for which $\dfrac{a}{b} + \dfrac{c}{d} = \dfrac{a+c}{b+d}$?

Problem: The shuttle service has a train going from New York to Boston and from Boston to New York every hour on the hour. The trip from one city to the other takes 4½ hours. How many of the Boston to New York trains will pass you on your trip from New York to Boston if you leave New York at 9:00?

Problem: Samantha wants to pile grapefruits in a store display in the form of a pyramid. She places 1 grapefruit on the top layer, 4 grapefruits on the second layer, 9 in the third layer, 16 in the fourth layer, and so on. If she uses all 385 grapefruits, how many layers will she have?

SECTION E

Masters for
Strategy Game Boards

Triangular Tic-Tac-Toe

Triangular Tic-Tac-Toe

Put 'Em Down Tic-Tac-Toe

Put 'Em Down Tic-Tac-Toe

Point Score Tic-Tac-Toe

Point Score Tic-Tac-Toe

Dots-in-a-Row Tic-Tac-Toe

Dots-in-a-Row Tic-Tac-Toe

Tac-Tic-Toe

Tac-Tic-Toe

Tac-Tic-Toe, Chinese Version

Tac-Tic-Toe, Chinese Version

Blockade

Blockade

Hex

Hex

Triahex

Triahex

Solitaire

Solitaire

Spot

Spot

Fox and Geese

Fox and Geese

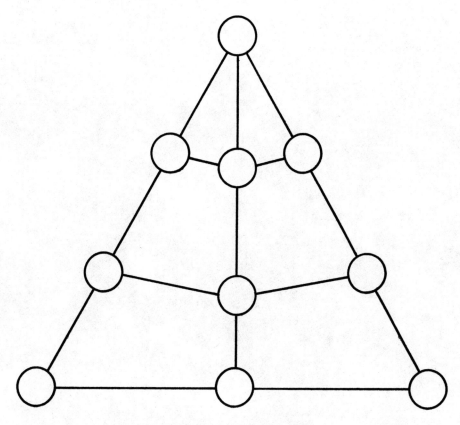

The Wolf and the Farmers

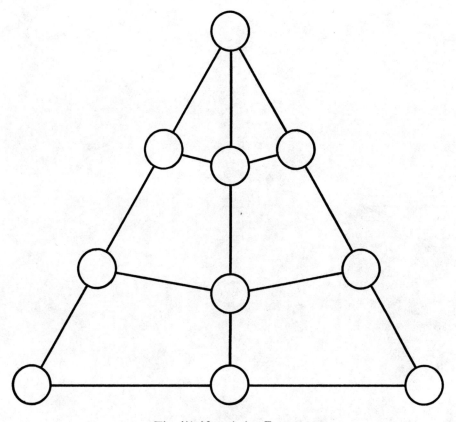

The Wolf and the Farmers